CLEAN PLATES

Brooklyn 2012

A Guide to the
Healthiest Tastiest
and Most Sustainable
Restaurants for Vegetarians
and Carnivores

By JARED KOCH

Reviews by

SARAH AMANDOLARE, TALIA BERMAN, JESSICA COLLEY,

JACLYN EINIS, ALLIX GENESLAW, DEBBIE KOENIG,

SCARLETT LINDEMAN, MEGAN MURPHY, AMY SUNG

DISCLAIMER: I am not a medical doctor, and nothing in this book is intended to diagnose, treat or cure any medical condition, illness or disease. Anyone with a specific medical condition should consult a physician.

Published by Craving Wellness
Cliffside Park, NJ

Cover design by Jessica Arana
Interior design by Gary Robbins

Printed in Canada

10   9   8   7   6   5   4   3   2   1

*Library of Congress
Cataloging-in-Publication Data:*

Koch, Jared.
    Clean Plates Brooklyn : a guide to the
    healthiest tastiest and most sustainable
    restaurants for vegetarians and
    carnivores / by Jared Koch et. al. –
    Cliffside Park, NJ : Craving Wellness,
    2011.
    p.   cm.
    ISBN 978-0-9821862-5-1
    1. Food—Popular works.
    2. Diet—Popular works.
    3. Nutrition—Popular works.
    4. Restaurants—New York (State)
        —New York.
    I. Title.
TX355.K63   2011
641—dc22
2008940260

CONTENTS

DESIGN YOUR OWN DIET

THE RESTAURANTS

ACKNOWLEDGMENTS

My deepest gratitude, appreciation and respect to the following people, without whom this book would not exist:

To all the chefs and restaurant owners dedicated to serving delicious but healthier food. A special thanks to Dan Barber, Bill Telepan, Sarma Melngailis, Debbie Covenagh, Amy Chaplin, Rene Duran, Melissa O'Donnell and Michael Anthony for taking the time to be interviewed.

Angela Starks and Bunny Wong for all their help writing and editing the nutritional content. Sarah Amandolare, Talia Berman, Jessica Colley, Jaclyn Einis, Allix Geneslaw, Debbie Koenig, Scarlett Lindeman, Megan Murphy, and Amy Sung for writing great reviews.

Jessica Arana for designing the logo and the book cover. Gary Robbins for interior design and layout. The whole gang at Monaco Lange for all of their invaluable suggestions.

Special thanks to Blake Appleby for always supporting, encouraging and inspiring me and offering her insightful opinions. To all my family, friends, teachers and clients who have contributed and enriched my life in so many significant ways. Greg Monaco for his talents, perspective and calm demeanor and for his invaluable advice every step of the way.

To Maji Chien, Niles Brooks Leuthold, and Laura Mordas-Schenkein for all of their invaluable help and dedication.

And to Mat Zucker, Lynnda Pollio, Yvonne Roehler at Jenkins Group, Kate Basrat, Ameet Maturu, Susan Banzon, Amy Bush, Angela Davis, Chad Thompson, Sam Rosen at ThoughtLead, Peter Horjus, Vera Svezia, Barry Flemming, Jeremy Funston, Lisa Vasher, Catherine Cusamano, Mark Sclafani, Katherine Jamieson, Kathleen Spinelli, Erin Turner, Michael Ellisberg, Nancy Weiser, Carey Peters, Brett Lavender, Cassandra Caffaltas, Kim Blozie and especially Andrew Cohen and everyone at EnlightenNext.

A NOTE FROM JARED

WELCOME TO CLEAN PLATES BROOKLYN 2012. For those of you already familiar with *Clean Plates Manhattan*, we hope you're as excited as we are to venture into Brooklyn. If this is your first experience with Clean Plates, welcome!

Our first Brooklyn edition features over 100 of the healthiest, tastiest, and most sustainable restaurants in this up-and-coming food mecca. We've teamed up with some talented local Brooklyn writers including Jaclyn Einis, Debbie Koenig, Sarah Amandolare, and Amy Sung. This edition also features reviews from our beloved Manhattan writers, including Talia Berman, Scarlett Lindeman and Allix Geneslaw alongside two new critics, Megan Murphy and Jessica Colley.

Eating healthier does not have to be challenging. Especially in Brooklyn. Especially with this book. In fact, it can be an easy, pleasurable and sacrifice-free adventure. I've created this book for you—for New Yorkers and Brooklynites—with exactly that in mind.

Let's face it: We dine out a lot. And restaurants can be bad-eating minefields. Then again, who would say no if a delicious antibiotic- and hormone-free steak or a plate of tasty organic vegetables materialized in front of them? No one actually *wants* to consume hormones, antibiotics or pesticides. It's just that searching for the good stuff takes time. Fortunately, it's been done for you, and with a one-two punch: every featured selection in *Clean Plates Brooklyn* is a restaurant that offers both delicious *and* nutritious fare. Rest assured because all were personally visited and screened by myself, a nutritional consultant, along with one of our talented food critics.

This book is about helping you make better, more informed choices. In fact, it's my intention that you actually will *crave* healthier food after reading it. You'll learn that there's more than one right way to eat—a theory called bio-individuality (Makes sense, right? After all, do you wear the same clothes as all of your friends? Why should food be any different?). Sure, there's a lot of nutritional information out there, but talk about confusing. That's why this guide provides an easy-to-follow education about the most important foods you will encounter when dining out. That way, you can use your knowledge to implement the life-changing diet that's right for *you*.

---

3 WAYS YOU CAN USE THIS BOOK

- To find healthy tastier and healthier restaurants in your area.
- To learn how to change your eating habits when you dine out—and in.
- To transform your life by seeing how eating healthier can be pleasurable and startlingly simple.

By now you're probably asking yourself: Who *is* this guy? Why should I listen to anything he says? Well, honestly, I'm not that different from you. I want to be healthy so I can enjoy my life and contribute to making the world a better place. Rather than bore you with a long report about my life (you can learn more by visiting cleanplates.com), I'll touch on a few highlights for your peace of mind.

After deferring my acceptance to medical school for a decade-long stint as a successful entrepreneur, I decided that I needed to figure out my health and happiness. As part of that journey, I not only became a certified nutritional consultant, yoga instructor and health coach but also healed myself from chronic irritable bowel syndrome (IBS), fatigue and skin issues. I'm now a nutritional consultant backed by eight years of immersing myself in the formal study of nutrition—and five years of working with clients. I've had some amazing teachers: Andrew Weil, M.D., Deepak Chopra and Walter Willett, the head of nutrition at Harvard, in addition to many experts in the fields of Raw Foods, Chinese Medicine, Ayurveda, Macrobiotics, Vegetarianism and High-Protein Diets.

For my clients, and in this book, I synthesize those dietary theories in an easy-to-use format—always keeping an open mind to discovering the truth about what actually works for each individual.

Thanks to my experiences, I've had several insights over the years about how we eat, all of which I will be sharing in more detail in *Clean Plates Brooklyn*:

- Eating well is the easiest and best way (along with exercise and perhaps meditation) to positively affect your health and improve your quality of life.
- Contrary to conventional wisdom, healthy eating can be enjoyable and satisfying, free from the typical guilt and confusion we usually feel in relation to eating.
- No single way of eating works for everyone, but there is a healthy way to eat that's just right for *you* and your body.
- A quick way to upgrade your well-being: Select higher-quality versions of whatever foods you're currently consuming, especially when it comes to animal-based products.
- To increase nutrient intake and boost immunity, start with food that's fresh (locally grown), non-toxic (organic) and mostly plant-based (more vegetables, fruits, nuts and seeds). Think of it as a tasty trio—local non-toxic plants.
- Reducing your intake of artificial, chemical-laden processed foods, as well as sugar, caffeine and alcohol, will have you feeling better immediately.
- Making small improvements over time leads to significant change.
- What's good for you is usually good for the environment. Growing food locally means less energy consumption. Organic items don't poison the earth. And a reduction in the demand for livestock frees up vital resources.
- It's entirely possible to commit to values of health and conscious consumerism *and* fully enjoy the pleasures of life and this wonderful city. Why? Because, increasingly, tasty and healthy food is accessible to everyone from vegans to carnivores.

One of the major reasons I wrote this book is that there's a real lack of helpful, well-organized information for people who wish to dine out mindfully and still enjoy the experience of eating. Sure, cooking at home is important and many nutrition books offer delicious recipes, but the truth is, we New Yorkers eat out a lot—it is part of the culture. Our city boasts amazing chefs and a stunning variety of cuisines; if you live here, it's likely that restaurants are where you get a huge proportion of your nourishment. During my preliminary investigations, I noted a few gaps in the advice offered by other books and websites: 1) It's easy to find places that list vegan and vegetarian establishments—but none adequately distinguish which spots are healthy (not all are) or which would be appealing for non-vegetarians. 2) Few are dedicated to omnivores who would like to frequent places that serve organic, local and sustainably-raised animal products, and those that do exist tend to be confusing, poorly researched, and neither comprehensive, nor screened for taste. That's why I created *Clean Plates* to be the most exceptionally well-researched, comprehensive and easy-to-use guide that exists; I'm certain it will help you navigate the ever-expanding maze of Brooklyn's healthiest, tastiest and most sustainable restaurants.

The main inspiration for this book, however, grew out of my interactions with my clients. Several years ago, I began researching "healthy restaurants" because I believed that I could both eat healthier and enjoy the pleasures and diversity of this wonderful city. As I shared my ever-growing list of healthier restaurants with my clients, they actually started implementing changes and feeling better—a fact that inspired me to thoroughly expand my research, hire an amazing food critic, and set out to create *Clean Plates*. I learned from counseling clients that real change calls for practical tools. I think of this book as one of those significant tools.

This project is an extension of the work that I do with my clients: a way to reach more people and contribute to a growing awareness of healthy, responsible and sustainable eating. Together, let's shatter the myth that healthier eating is a sacrifice and prove that we can do it without the guilt, inconvenience, boredom and sheer lack of long-term success that characterize the usual diets.

You see, eating clean food is admirable, but I am equally interested in clean plates—the kind of food that makes you want to lick your dishes.

In good health,

Jared Koch

HOW TO USE THIS BOOK

JUST AS THERE'S NO one-size-fits-all diet for everyone, there's no
one right way to read and use this book. But I'd like to point out several
helpful features.

Take It With You Everywhere

Constructed to be small and lightweight, *Clean Plates Brooklyn* is easy
to slip in a bag or back pocket, and its rounded corners will keep it from
getting dog-eared. No matter where you are in Brooklyn, you'll be able
to quickly locate a restaurant that serves a healthy, delicious version of
the cuisine you're in the mood for—from fast food to fine dining, vegan
to omnivore and any combination thereof. Don't want to keep it on you?
Another option is to store one at home and one at the office (hey, I won't
stop you from buying two—the price has been kept low to make the
book accessible to as many people as possible).

Learn More About Healthier Eating

Take a peek at the sections of the book preceding the restaurant
reviews, where I lay out my *Five Precepts for Eating Well*. In those
sections I provide an easy-to-follow education on the pros and cons
of all the different foods you're likely to encounter at restaurants.
From beef to milk to cheese to less-known items like kefir, I've got you
covered. Due to the guide's size and scope, it's not a comprehensive
list or discussion but rather a very strong foundation from which
you can make intelligent and informed choices. Armed with my *Five
Precepts* and a clear understanding of different foods, you'll be able to
implement healthier eating habits immediately.

Find the Healthy Restaurant You Want with Easy-to-Use Listings

I don't want anyone to be left out. So whether you're a vegetarian, vegan
or meat-eater—and whether you want to spend lavishly or lightly—
I've tracked down restaurants for you (always serving delicious meals,

naturally). *Clean Plates Brooklyn* boasts an incredibly diverse array of over 100 establishments (including full reviews) representing all manner of cuisines, budgets and geographic locations. Among many other options, you'll find (a) the best-tasting hormone and antibiotic-free animal products; (b) the best-tasting high-quality vegetarian dishes; and (c) the best-tasting naturally sweetened desserts.

Find a Restaurant Quickly Using the Index

The index offers a way to quickly reference what you are looking for in a variety of different configurations from geography to brunch options to top date spots.

Discover How Eating Well Can Be Fun, Guilt-Free and Life-Changing

I like to think of this book as a tool. It gives you the information you need to eat healthier—with little effort, since the book does the work for you—and puts to rest the excuse that healthy foods are too inaccessible and expensive to incorporate into your life. And then there's the domino effect: when you crave better food and eat more of it, your body responds, rewarding you with better moods, energy and health.

Save the World While You're At It

As a nutritional consultant and health coach, I believe in caring for the world around you—an attitude that can become the impetus for environmentally beneficial actions like selecting organic, local food.

RESTAURANT REVIEW PROCESS AND CRITERIA

THIS BOOK IS MEANT to be an indispensable resource for your real-life needs: it's practical, easy to use, easy to follow...and life changing. Yes, life changing. Because if you start eating at several of the restaurants we recommend, I can almost guarantee that you'll feel better, become healthier and begin to crave food that's good for you.

Maybe you're a vegetarian with a meat-eating, foodie spouse. Or a workaholic who orders in takeout at the office. Or perhaps you're both. No matter what, this book features a restaurant for you. In fact it has a restaurant for nearly every permutation of taste, cuisine and geographic preference: upscale and fast food, from Williamsburg to Flatbush, Korean and Italian, vegetarian, vegan, meat-serving and much more.

There are only two constants. Every single featured restaurant serves *delicious* and *nutritious* dishes. How'd we find them? In the next several paragraphs, I explain.

Why We Used Food Critics and a Nutritionist

Eating healthy foods is considerably more appealing when you enjoy what you're eating, yet most health-food guides give scant attention to taste. Not this one. This one should please the most critical, severe and discerning of foodies. How can I be sure? Well, after interviewing several seasoned writers, I selected and worked with the very talented Clean Plates writers, such as Jaclyn Einis, Talia Berman and Jessica Colley to sift through the potential contenders (for bios on all of our writers, visit www.cleanplates.com). Each critic had to visit and review every restaurant as far as taste goes; if she didn't think it served delicious food, it didn't make it into this book. And as a nutritional consultant, I screened and approved every spot to make sure its meals were healthy. How can you be certain you're going to get a healthy *and* delicious meal? Just eat at any of the restaurants featured in *Clean Plates Brooklyn*.

How We Found the Restaurants

My goal was to compile a list of healthy local restaurants that accommodated both vegetarians and carnivores and was as wide-ranging as possible. From there, the food critics and I would whittle it down to the very best. I already had a small file of such establishments, assembled over the years; I added to it by tracking down healthy eateries in every way possible. I read other guidebooks, searched online, asked restaurant owners, petitioned my friends and literally walked and drove around the city looking for places. The result: a master list of a couple hundred restaurants. True, I may have missed a few—this is Brooklyn, after all, home to a dizzying array of eateries; plus, before now, there hasn't been a good resource for vegetarians and especially carnivores seeking healthy but tasty foods. In fact, that's one of the reasons why I also set up a website (cleanplates.com) where you can stay up-to-date, share your opinions, and give and receive information about closings and openings.

The Screening, Researching, Reviewing and Fact-Checking Process

First, I subjected each place on our master list of several hundred restaurants to a health-screening process. Posing as a potential customer over the phone, the *Clean Plates* team and I queried the staff about their preparation and sourcing methods (examples: Is your meat hormone- and antibiotic-free? Is it grass-fed? What is your apple pie sweetened with? Do you use a microwave?). In addition, I thoroughly reviewed the menu online or in person.

If the restaurant passed this initial health test, I sent one of my trusted food critics to visit it incognito (so that she wouldn't receive special treatment). She ordered as wide a variety of foods as possible—appetizers, side dishes, main courses and desserts—and didn't just stick to her own taste. In addition, she asked the staff more questions, some a repeat of what we had asked on the phone (more examples: Is your water filtered? Is your produce local and organic?).

Next, the food critic and I discussed whether the restaurant met our taste and health criteria. After we selected a restaurant, I or someone on my team called to inform them about their inclusion in this book and have an owner, manager or chef fill out a survey to fact-check the details.

Our Criteria

We struggled between being selective and comprehensive and, in the end, decided it was important to offer a hybrid of both. When choosing a restaurant, we took the following areas into consideration:

- Taste
- Atmosphere
- Type of cuisine: We wanted to make sure a wide variety of cuisines were included, from pizza and burgers to Caribbean and French foods, and on and on. And we added extra points for accessibility, such as when a vegetarian restaurant had a menu that most carnivores would enjoy or when a carnivore-friendly place offered several vegetarian options.
- Lifestyle: To ensure that personal tastes and needs were met, we included casual, power lunch, and fine dining establishments, as well as those that are family-friendly and date-worthy—and more. Even if you occasionally crave fast-food, we have you covered (and that's *healthier* fast-food, naturally).
- Geography: Wherever you find yourself in Brooklyn—wherever you live, work, shop and hang out—we've identified a restaurant nearby that serves healthy and delicious meals.
- Healthfulness of ingredients: All of our restaurants that serve animal products source, at the very least, almost entirely (if not entirely) from farms raising animals without the use of hormones or antibiotics.
  In addition, we awarded points for restaurants that:
- Source grass-fed, organic, free-range animals
- Order from small, local farms
- Include a high percentage of vegetables on the menu

- Purchase produce from organic or local purveyors
- Filter their water
- Use high-quality salts
- Offer naturally sweetened desserts
- Include organic and biodynamic wines and organic coffees on their menu
- Sell better quality soda and soft drinks
- Have wheat- and gluten-free options

We deducted points from restaurants that:
- Offer animal foods that weren't sustainably raised
- Use too many fake soy products
- Have too much seitan, a wheat-gluten product used as a fake-meat substitute
- Don't include enough vegetable options or greens on the menu
- Follow poor-quality cooking methods, such as frying
- Cook with poor-quality oils
- Overemphasize dairy, shellfish, veal and foie gras

Our Featured Selections: Clean Plates Approved!

In alphabetical order, the best restaurants (over 100)—the places that passed our taste and health tests with very high scores—are given informative and entertaining reviews by one of our food critics. For easier browsing, we include icons that provide key information (is it vegetarian? Does it serve animal foods? Is it a good budget pick?).

If you simply stick to eating at a combination of these restaurants when you dine out, there's a good chance that you'll improve your quality of life and your health. Why? Well, for one thing, you'll be putting better foods into your body, and it will respond in kind. For another, you'll start to associate delicious meals with healthy meals—and you'll begin to crave the latter. In fact, consuming junk food will seem less and less appealing. And you'll be doing all of this with little effort because the restaurants—and this book—will have done the work for you. All you have to do is eat!

Visit Cleanplates.com

In addition to the restaurants featured in this book, on our website we also include what I like to call the Honorable Mentions: restaurants that didn't quite meet all of our criteria. They are divided into two categories: one is of eateries that passed our health tests but not our taste tests; we visited all of these places and call them "healthy not as tasty". The other is of establishments that didn't pass our health tests; some of these we visited, and they served delicious food but just weren't healthy enough. In other cases we didn't visit the restaurant because it didn't pass our initial health screening, but we included them because they're doing a better than average job using healthier and more sustainable ingredients. We call them "tasty not as healthy". You do need to be more discerning at these establishments, but they are better for you than the typical New York City restaurant.

Other great reasons to visit cleanplates.com:

- Sign up for updates on new restaurant openings and closings
- Get notified of restaurant promotions and offerings
- Read interviews with health-conscious and sustainable-savvy chefs
- Create a user profile and share your comments and experiences at Clean Plates-approved restaurants
- Browse menus
- Order delivery via SeamlessWeb
- Reserve a table through OpenTable
- Stay informed with healthier eating tips and the latest in nutrition and sustainable food news
- Follow us on Twitter and "like" us on Facebook.
- Learn more about the *Clean Plates* mobile version

WHY EAT HEALTHIER?

For Physical Health and Quality of Life

FINANCIAL COLUMNISTS LIKE TO point out that ordering a $3 latte every day adds up to $1,000 a year that otherwise would have been accruing interest in a CD. Our daily food choices operate according to similar principles; instead of building up our financial assets, however, we are building our health resources.

Several cases in point: You wake up, yawning, get dressed, and (a) start the day with a cup of herbal tea or glass of water with lemon to accompany your bowl of oatmeal and fruit; or (b) pick up a Starbucks coffee with sugar on your way to work, skipping breakfast. Later the same day, you and your co-workers order out for (a) wild salmon with vegetables and brown rice; or (b) fast-food hamburgers and fries. You get the picture: Going for the "b" option day in and day out adds up to nothing good, while repeated "a" choices equals a lifetime of overall optimal well-being.

That's why we should remind ourselves why it's worth it to be healthy (typically, better looks, lower weight!). But how about more energy, feeling better, lower healthcare bills, and even better sex. So think about those benefits the next time you're tempted by the often-insidious forces that affect our food choices, like instant gratification, biochemical addiction, emotional and peer pressure, and just plain old habit.

Our health may be affected more by the foods we eat than by any other factor. I think that's great news, since it means we can do something about it. Of course, exercise, sleep and genetics—not to mention our relationships, career and spirituality—count, too. But the reason "you are what you eat" has endured as a phrase is because what we consume builds, fuels, cleanses or—unfortunately—pollutes our very cells.

At the end of the day, it all comes down to choices.

For the World Beyond Your Plate

Here's a new one: an organic apple a day keeps the greenhouse gases away. Translation? Eating naturally is good for nature. It's not only physical health that inspires me to be conscious about what I eat—it's also the environment. Here's a list of simple ways to positively affect the planet through your food choices.

1. CUT DOWN ON ANIMAL PRODUCTS.

No need to go vegetarian to reduce your impact. But consuming less meat—poultry, beef, fish, dairy and eggs—is a powerful way to help the earth. I hope the following facts motivate you to skip a main course of meat or dine at a vegetarian restaurant now and then, even if you're an omnivore.

- Wasted water. Beef is one of the worst offenders; its production in the United States alone requires more water than growing the world's fruit and vegetable crop.
- Wasted land. Livestock consume grain that uses up many acres.
- Wasted energy. It takes ten times more fossil fuel to produce a meat-based diet than a plant-based one. That statistic led the United Nations to declare "Raising animals for food generates more greenhouse gases than all the cars and trucks in the world combined."

• Wasteful, er, waste. Don't picture this while you're eating, but imagine the amount of sewage generated by farm animals, which comprise three times the number of humans on the planet.

2. STOCK UP ON ORGANIC FOODS.

More toxic than ever before, pesticides and herbicides contaminate the soil, water and air which in turn poison both humans and wildlife. So support restaurants that source organic products or suggest that your favorite local eatery consider purchasing from Certified Naturally Grown Farms (certifiednaturallygrown.org), an organization that exceeds USDA organic standards and is locally based in upstate New York.

> **TIP: A WORD OF CAUTION**
>
> Just because locally grown and organic foods are better for the environment doesn't mean they're always healthier for our bodies. Locally grown organic sugar? Sorry, still sugar to your body.

3. GO YIMBY (YES IN MY BACKYARD) BY CHOOSING LOCALLY GROWN FOODS.

Most food travels from the farm to the restaurant on a long-distance trek, gobbling up fuel and requiring environmentally damaging packaging. As Stephen Hopp says in his wife Barbara Kingsolver's book *Animal, Vegetable, Miracle*, "If every U.S. citizen ate just one meal a week composed of locally and organically raised meats and produce, we would reduce our country's oil consumption by over 1.1 million barrels of oil every week."

4. AVOID GMOS.

The name certainly doesn't sound healthy: genetically modified organisms, aka GMOs. These artificially altered crops require an enormous amount of pesticides (they even produce pesticides within their own cells), and they cross-contaminate other crops and harm wildlife. The majority of soy (as in tofu), corn and canola crops are now GMO plants; if these items are staples in your diet, frequent eateries that serve organic versions.

5. SAY SAYONARA TO BOTTLED WATER.

Americans use two million plastic bottles *every five minutes*. Imagine them all stacked up in a pile. The amount of oil needed to make those bottles equals about 15 million barrels a year. Even recycling them means using more fossil fuels. Opt for filtered water when available and encourage restaurant owners to invest in a filtration system.

WHAT'S MORE IMPORTANT: LOCALLY GROWN OR ORGANIC?

Organic but non-local produce is free of pesticides harmful to our bodies and the soil but requires extra energy to travel from farm to table and loses nutrients along the way. *Locally Grown* but non-organic goods retain most of their nutrients because of the speed at which they get to our plates, but they may be sprayed with chemicals, which are damaging to our bodies, the soil and the atmosphere. *The answer:* Unfortunately, if you can't get an item locally grown and organic, there is no easy answer. It is a matter of personal choice and if you choose one or the other you are doing pretty good.

DESIGN YOUR OWN DIET

I BELIEVE THERE *IS* a dream diet for everyone—it's just not the same for each person. That brings me to a key principle of this book:

THE FIRST PRECEPT: There's more than one right way to eat.

As nutrition pioneer Roger Williams writes in his groundbreaking 1950s book *Biochemical Individuality*, "If we continue to try to solve problems on the basis of the average man, we will be continually in a muddle. Such a man does not exist."

We're all biochemically—genetically, hormonally and so on—different, and the idea that this should guide our eating habits has recently begun to excite the leading-edge medical and nutrition community. Experts are beginning to talk about the benefits of individualizing our diets rather than giving advice based on recommended daily allowances (RDA) or the United States Department of Agriculture's (USDA's) food pyramid, both created with the "average" person in mind.

How We Differ

As you read through my list of how we're all unique, some of the points may seem obvious (of course someone training for a marathon requires different foods than someone sitting in front of a computer all day, for instance). But part of what I'd like to get across is that these distinctions manifest themselves not only between individuals, but also between your different selves—your tired self, your active self and the like. The key is to pay attention to how your body reacts to various foods and to what it's telling you at any given moment.

- Genetic Makeup: To a large extent, the anatomy and body chemistry that you inherited from your ancestors determine your nutritional needs and ability to benefit from particular foods. For example, a few recent studies have shown that some people possess the genetic ability to metabolize caffeine more efficiently than others. Research has also revealed that specific groups of people have the genetic makeup to absorb vitamin B12 with ease, or benefit greatly from broccoli's cancer-fighting nutrients—while others lack those genes.

- Culture and Background: Your ethnicity and upbringing influence how your body acts. For instance, several of my friends have inherited a genetic ability enabling them to drink milk, but my friend who is Asian is lactose intolerant, as are many of his compatriots—his grandparents came to America from a country where milk rarely makes it onto the menu. So it's helpful to consider which foods are part of your culture and background, and incorporate the appropriate ones into your diet.
- Lifestyle: A man training for a marathon requires different foods than a person who does an hour of yoga each week.
- Day-to-day physical health: Pay attention to your physical health symptoms to figure out what foods you need. Sick? Miso soup may be just the thing. Sneezing constantly? Avoid dairy and sugar; the former causes the body to produce mucus and the latter weakens the immune system.
- Gender: Whether you're a man or a woman affects your diet needs. For example, menstruating women require more iron than men, but men need more zinc than their female counterparts to nourish their reproductive systems.
- Age: A growing, active teen will be ravenous at dinnertime; the same person, 60 years later, will likely find that his appetite is waning.
- Seasons and Climate: Even the weather affects what's best for you to eat. When it's hot outside, the body will likely crave cooling foods like salads; on a cold winter day, hot soup is more appealing.

Eating as a Bio-Individual

The philosophy that no single way of eating is right for everyone isn't new. Both Traditional Chinese Medicine and India's Ayurvedic system revolve around prescribing the most appropriate diet for specific categories of body types and constitutions.

More recent incarnations of these ancient approaches include the blood-type diet and metabolic typing. The blood-type diet was made famous a decade ago by naturopath Peter D'Adamo, who theorized (to put it very simply) that people with blood type O do best eating meat, but type A's thrive as vegetarians. The thinking behind the discovery? Type O's descended from ancient hunters while type A's came from agricultural civilizations. The idea behind metabolic typing (again, to put it simply) is that your metabolism dictates the appropriate percentage of proteins or carbohydrates in your diet; those who metabolize proteins well require extra animal foods, while others do better with more carbs.

Not everyone agrees. Proponents of *The China Study*, a 2005 book by two nutritional biochemists who conducted a 20-year survey of Chinese diets, argue that animal consumption is the leading cause of human disease, while followers of Weston A. Price, a dentist who carried out extensive health research in many countries, rely on culturally based studies to back up their claim that animal proteins and organ meats have benefits. Ultimately, the jury is still out (and probably always will be) on whether we have evolved to be omnivores or vegetarians. Though I do believe in the importance of our culture moving more toward a vegetarian-based diet, I have also observed that, while some people thrive on a vegetarian or vegan diet, others do not—some people require (high-quality) animal protein to function optimally.

HOW SHOULD YOU APPROACH OTHER DIETARY THEORIES?

One diet (it's pushing it to call it a dietary theory!) that most of us would like to move away from is the standard American diet (or SAD, as I call it). So what should we move toward? Well, we all have different needs, but that doesn't mean we have to invent diets from scratch. We have help: Other established dietary theories. It's worth knowing about them, so you can consider which parts of each work for you.

For instance, if you're energetic, enjoy a challenge and possess a strong digestive system, you fit the description of a good candidate for raw foodism. It's a relatively new diet based on ancient principles in which vegetables, fruits, nuts and seeds are served uncooked—or heated to a maximum of 118 degrees Fahrenheit in order to maintain nutrients and enzymes. Fit the description but balking at consuming only uncooked foods? Maybe partial raw foodism is right for you (say, 50 percent raw and 50 percent cooked). Or perhaps you're eager to transition away from junk food or dairy and are very disciplined and love Asian food to boot; in that case, a macrobiotic diet may be right for you. It's a route that heavily emphasizes rice, however, so it's not the best choice for someone who doesn't do well on grains. And for many people, considering vegetarianism makes sense. If you do decide to experiment with not eating meat, be sure to avoid the pitfalls that many vegans and vegetarians accidentally step into—namely, eating too many processed foods, carbohydrates, dairy and sugar, as well as consuming too much soy in the form of fake-meat products.

Still confused? Think of it as designing your own diet using bits and pieces of good, but different, ideas. The point is that you don't need to adhere to any particular theory (they all have their pros and cons and none are right for everyone). Instead, tailor what you eat to your biology, body, blood type, hormones, tastes and way of looking at the world. My next four precepts will help to guide your choices.

How We're the Same

Our food choices often become another way of separating us. When there are moral underpinnings to our choices, it's especially tempting to think that "my way is the only right way to eat." What I like most about bio-individuality is that the focus is on how our physical selves can achieve their fullest potential. In my opinion, when that happens—when we're able to thrive physically—we've created an unshakable foundation for living to our fullest potential and for making a meaningful contribution to our collective well-being as a species and a planet.

Being different should bring us together. Why? Well, partially because it's about realizing that other people have needs distinct from ours. Some types love to begin their day with a shot of wheatgrass—but perhaps the thought makes you turn green. And while your friends can't imagine living without an occasional hamburger or slice of pizza, you might thrive on hearty salads and raw foods. And we all know that irritating person who can gobble up everything in sight and remain slim—a profile that many of us don't have. Hopefully being aware of these distinctions will lead us to be less critical of others—and less likely to feel guilty about our own choices. Judgment and guilt, after all, are bad for your health. At the very least, they really mess with your digestion.

BIO-INDIVIDUALITY MEANS THAT THERE'S no perfect diet for everyone. There *is*, however, the perfect food for everyone—real food. It's what we're designed to eat, regardless of our lifestyle, genetic makeup and other differences. Which leads me to my next premise.

THE SECOND PRECEPT: The overwhelming majority of your diet should consist of natural, high-quality and whole foods.

Which means...what? What, exactly, is real food? It's a question I often get from my clients. Once upon a time, it had an obvious answer, but, over the past hundred years, food has become increasingly unlike itself: processed, altered with chemicals, dyed unnatural colors, flavored with suspect ingredients and generally turned as artificial as can be.

These kinds of changes generally result in more toxins and fewer nutrients. In my opinion, the success of diets like macrobiotics and raw foods in claiming to help heal diabetes and even cancer (according to some studies) is due in large part to the fact that both diets call for increasing your intake of real, high quality, whole foods while reducing consumption of artificial and chemical-laden dishes.

TIP: DON'T GET SIDETRACKED BY FOCUSING ONLY ON CALORIES

Many people equate reducing calories with a healthier lifestyle, but I firmly believe that the quality of the foods we eat are much more important—even when it comes to losing weight. Here's a way of looking at it: Think of food as fuel. Does a car run best on poor-quality fuel? No, of course not. And our bodies are the same: They need optimal fuel. Another way of looking at it is to ask yourself: What's better for my body—1,800 calories of junk food and candy bars, or 2,000 calories of vegetables and fruits? I think you get the idea!

All this means we desperately need to get back to basics. To help you with the terms (high quality, whole, natural) and to give you an answer to the question above (What, exactly, is real food?), read on.

Real, aka Natural

In this book, I use the terms *real* and *natural* synonymously, a fact that may help you distinguish real from artificial. Knowing what's natural is largely a matter of intuition and common sense; it's not as if you're going to start bringing a checklist to restaurants.

Nevertheless, you'll become a pro at identifying the real thing more quickly if you ask yourself a couple of questions the next time you eat. These questions include: What would I eat if I lived in the wild? What has the earth and nature provided for humans to eat? What have I, as a human, evolved to eat? To keep it simple, focus on what grows out of the ground or on a tree. In addition, think vegetables, fruits, nuts, seeds, beans, grains, herbs and animal foods.

TIP: AN EASY WAY TO FIGURE OUT IF IT'S REAL FOOD

Just ask yourself this question: Was it made in nature or in a factory? Visualize where the item began its life. Perhaps you'll see it hanging on a bush, growing on a tree, sprouting up from the earth or grazing in a field. If it's fizzing to life in a test tube, move on.

Quality

A peach from the grocery store is a real-food item—it was made in nature and wasn't flavored in a factory—but that doesn't mean it's the best quality. The more of the following qualities the peach has, the higher its quality: it's organic, with fewer chemicals and more nutrients than its non-organic counterpart; locally grown, so it requires less artificial ripening and storage and loses fewer nutrients en route from farm to plate; non-irradiated, since radiation destroys nutrients and changes an item's chemical structure; and not genetically modified (non-GMO), an unnatural process with unknown consequences.

In addition, ask yourself if additives, flavorings, coloring or preservatives were used. It's not always obvious in a restaurant, but it's worth considering. For instance, a cupcake with fire-engine red icing probably has, among other things, icing that's artificially colored.

Whole

This term is about processes and cooking methods: The fewer things done to a food, the better. Basically, cooking and preparing food makes it less whole—but that doesn't necessarily mean the dish in question is unhealthy.

Raw foods (that is, uncooked) are in their natural state with their nutrients intact. Yet cooking is often considered the first step in the digestive process. Why? Well, it breaks down the food's cell walls and fiber, making it easier to absorb the food's nutrients. Although I am not typically a proponent of a 100% Raw-Food diet, I do believe that we should aim to eat a significant amount of raw foods as well as some cooked foods. The ratio will ultimately depend on the strength of your digestive system and personal tastes.

When examining the healthfulness of a prepared dish, you should consider:

- The cooking methods used. Err on the side of undercooking, since prolonged exposure to high heat destroys nutrients, enzymes and water content. Examples: Steaming or poaching (good) versus frying (not good) or microwaving (bad).
- The wholeness of the ingredients. Examples: A bowl of berries (good) versus fruit juice with sugar (not good).
- The number of steps or processes used to make the food. Examples: A bowl of oatmeal made from whole oats (good) versus cereal made into flakes (not so good).

What to Ask

Some establishments make meals from scratch, while others pre-make recipes in bulk and microwave them on demand. To find out whether your dish is real, quality and whole, ask the staff to confirm your meal's origins, ingredients and preparation techniques.

The kinds of questions you might have include whether brown rice can be substituted for white; if the cheese is raw or pasteurized; if the cakes are made with butter (real) or margarine (fake); whether the salmon is artificially colored or is the genuine wild-harvested article; and if the beef comes from a grass-fed cow or one fattened with grains, antibiotics and growth hormones.

I also like to know if the vegetables on my plate have just been steamed or whether the only kitchen tool required was a can opener. Peas from a can, for instance, often come with added salt. The same goes for fruit. Say there's a restaurant that lists peaches and cream on the dessert menu. Are those high-quality, real peaches or the kind that come out of a can (where they've been marinating in flavored-sugar syrup)?

A Word About Beverages

And don't forget the drinks. Is the water filtered or from the city's chlorinated supply? The former is actually closer to fresh, natural water. Is the soda sweetened with fruit juice or with high-fructose corn syrup? And that coffee—decaffeinated naturally?

Think of these ideas as practice exercises for your "food radar"—a muscle of sorts that will grow stronger with use. The more you check for the differences between whole and unwholesome, high quality and run-of-the-mill, real and processed, the more automatic eating real, whole and high-quality foods will become.

Foods For Thought

Fats, sweeteners, grains, animal products: They sound like basics, but they come in many guises—and are the cause of many debates. Take bread. Mom always told you it was an essential source of fiber, but your newspaper's science section just ran an article about how humans aren't designed to eat grains. At any rate, you're not going to forswear bread completely because you love it—but should you pair it with butter or with margarine? The latter, after all, contains fewer calories. But wasn't there a television report the other day about the evils of margarine?

The fact is, confusion and controversy surround many types of food—some more than others. To clear things up and to give you the tools to design your own diet, I've compiled information about various foods and food categories, from vegetables and fruits to meat and dairy. What you learn will enable you to make smart dietary choices.

WHAT I'M ABOUT TO SAY might be difficult to absorb—not because you've never heard it before, but rather because you've heard it, in some form, thousands of times. But let me tell you what it is, and then I'll address figuring out how to make it stick:

THE THIRD PRECEPT:
Everyone would be better off if a larger proportion of their diet consisted of plants—mostly vegetables (in particular, leafy greens), along with some nuts, seeds and fruits.

To get this message to sink in, I encourage clients to think about it in big, overarching terms. I like to point out that eating plants is a way of taking in the energy of the sun. As a life force, the sun contributes to our health and sense of well-being enormously. Without it there would be no life on earth. Want more of it? Eat more plants. They're a more direct source of "sun food" than meat; when we eat animals, we are indirectly consuming what they themselves already ate.

If this concept is a bit too esoteric, consider it from a scientific point of view. What gives green plants their color? It's chlorophyll, the pigment in leaves that enables them to absorb the sun's rays using a process called photosynthesis. Many nutritionists believe that when we eat green leaves, we take in that stored solar energy. Chlorophyll enriches blood, kills germs, detoxifies the bloodstream and liver, reduces bodily odors and controls the appetite.

Still snoozing off when you hear "eat more plants"? Maybe telling yourself, "I'll have more energy" will provide the necessary motivation instead.

To help you navigate between different types of plants, the following two sections of this book are devoted to information about vegetables and fruits. It's not wrong to eat meat—in fact, it can be healthy for certain people— but eat lots of plants, and you'll start to feel better. The next two sections show you why.

THINK ABOUT IT: YET ANOTHER REASON TO EAT VEGGIES

Have you ever heard of anyone being overweight or getting heart disease or cancer from eating too many vegetables?

Veggie Tales

Pity the unappreciated vegetable. Perpetually shunted to the side—as a garnish, appetizer, side dish—it rarely gets to give all that it has to offer. What does it offer, you ask? An enormous amount of nutrients and health-boosting properties in the form of vitamins, minerals, fiber, phytochemicals and antioxidants. Vegetables should form the bulk of your diet.

QUICK DEFINITION: ANTIOXIDANTS

Their name says it all: they're *anti*-oxidants. They counteract oxidation—and the free radicals believed to speed up aging and disease. A variety of elements cause our bodies to produce excess free radicals. Some are "bad," like toxic air and the chemicals to which we're exposed, but some are everyday, such as exercise and the normal process of metabolizing food for energy. Fortunately, you can combat these excess free radicals by eating more vegetables (as well as fruits, nuts and seeds), which are abundant in antioxidants.

If you're a vegetarian, aim to increase the proportion of veggies that you consume relative to the amount of grains, beans, dairy, sugar and tofu in your diet. Similarly, omnivores should be mindful of the meat-to-vegetable ratio in each meal.

And I'd like to take a moment to remind you about my second premise—eat high-quality, natural and whole vegetables. For one thing, they taste noticeably better. In addition, local, organic vegetables suffer less nutrient loss than their long-distance counterparts; they also reap the benefits of organic soils, which are rich in nutrients.

In addition, these do-it-all veggies possess a characteristic that many people don't know to look for but that's important for good health: they're alkalizing. In contrast, most foods in the standard American diet—especially meats, sugar and white flour—are acid-forming. Without getting into the nitty-gritty science of it, I'd like to point out that most disease states within the body occur in an acidic environment. Foods that create alkalinity are healthier.

To help you order at restaurants, here's a roundup of the types of vegetables you're likely to encounter—and how they affect your body:

QUICK TIP: SQUEEZE SOME LEMON IN YOUR WATER

A one-question quiz: Is a lemon acidic or alkalizing for the body? Well, even though lemons taste acidic, they're actually one of the most alkalizing foods as far as the chemistry they produce in your blood.

LEAFY GREENS should be a priority because they're one of the most nutrient-dense foods. Chock-full of chlorophyll, they also boast a calcium-to-magnesium ratio that makes them great bone builders and encourages relaxation and appropriate nerve-and-muscle responsiveness, ensuring the body's smooth functioning. And as well as being a good way to obtain iron, vitamin C and folic acid, leafy greens contain essential amino acids, meaning they're an excellent source of protein—one that potentially rivals the kind from animals. Let's take a look at some of the more common leafy greens.

Kale, swiss chard, collards and spinach are all chef favorites. If possible, ask for yours to be lightly steamed or even served raw, both options that retain more nutrients than frying. A quick sauté with garlic is another delicious and healthy alternative.

Spinach enjoys an impressive reputation (think Popeye) but contains oxalic acid, an anti-nutrient that prevents the absorption and use of calcium and may contribute to kidney stones and gout. While some nutritional experts insist that thorough cooking neutralizes the acid, others report that overcooking makes it toxic (the latter group suggest eating it raw). Until there's a definitive answer, I recommend enjoying spinach without overdoing it, and opting instead for kale, swiss chard or collard greens when possible.

Lettuce, mesclun greens, watercress and arugula often appear in salads, meaning they're raw and still contain all their nutrients and enzymes (watercress in particular is rich in B vitamins). But skip iceberg lettuce. The most common salad green in the United States, iceberg lettuce has few nutrients and tends to be heavily sprayed.

Parsley and dandelion greens, both highly nutritious, don't make it onto menus as often as other greens; when they do, it's usually as a garnish or as part of a salad. Parsley is incredibly rich in iron and

Drinking the juice of any type of green—not just wheatgrass—is a speedy way to get a nutrient infusion without your teeth or digestive system having to work at breaking down the plants' cell walls. Nevertheless, don't stop eating whole greens, since they provide fiber as well as some nutrients that may be lost or oxidized in the juicing process.

vitamin C, while bitter dandelion—an acquired taste—offers some vitamin D and helps to cleanse the liver.

Wheatgrass tends to conjure up images of earthy-crunchy types, but I think a better way to look at it is as a treat for health connoisseurs. It boasts one of the most concentrated sources of chlorophyll, a pigment (as you may recall from earlier) that captures the sun's energy and passes its healthful effects along to your body. New Yorkers knock it back like a shot of espresso at juice bars and health-food restaurants all over the city.

CRUCIFEROUS VEGETABLES are plants in the cabbage family, a category that includes broccoli, cauliflower, Brussels sprouts, kale, bok choy and all cabbages (yep, there's some overlap with the "leafy greens" group). High in vitamin C and soluble fiber, these foods also are crammed with nutrients boasting potent anti-cancer properties. And only cruciferous vegetables contain isothiocyanates, a nutrient that has been associated with a decrease in lung cancer.

These veggies crop up in all guises on menus, most often as a side (of broccoli or cauliflower, for instance), but sometimes in stir-fries and casseroles. And they're common at Asian and raw-food eateries, where items like broccoli or kale tend to be served raw and marinated—a preparation method that imparts a sautéed texture without the nutrient loss that comes with actual sautéing.

ROOT VEGETABLES include carrots, beets, potatoes, parsnips, yams, turnips and radishes, each with a unique nutritional profile. Carrots, for instance, contain the antioxidant known as betacarotene; beets, crammed with iron, enrich the blood. White potatoes, however, have more sugar and fewer nutrients than yams or sweet potatoes. When possible, inquire about substituting one of the latter two in potato-based dishes.

MUSHROOMS probably generate the most controversy of all vegetables, at least as far as their health claims go. Some nutritionists advise steering clear because they are, after all, fungus, and are therefore potentially infectious. They're also hard to digest. Other experts, however, particularly those who study Asian cultures, vaunt the medicinal properties of mushrooms. Personally, I like to stick to the shiitake and maitake (hen of the woods) varieties, both of which have cancer-fighting and immune-boosting properties (recent studies have suggested that button mushrooms contain several goodies such as antioxidants, too).

KIMCHI and **SAUERKRAUT** come in what is possibly the best form in which to consume your veggies—raw and fermented. Literally "alive," they teem with nutrients, enzymes and probiotics, which aid digestion.

As central to Korean culture as pasta is to Italy, kimchi may contain any type of vegetable but often includes cabbage and carrots, which are typically spiced up with garlic, ginger or cayenne. Because of its spiciness, kimchi makes not only a great snack, but also a delicious condiment. A German staple, sauerkraut is made from cultured cabbage. Both naturally fermented treats are becoming popular in all types of restaurants as a side dish, in sandwiches or as part of a main course.

QUICK DEFINITION: GOOD GERMS AND ENZYMES

We hear it constantly: such-and-such food boasts enzymes and probiotics. But what do those funny-sounding things do?

Enzymes control the rate of every chemical reaction in your system, which means that you need them to digest food. So what happens when we don't get our enzymes, which are potentially destroyed by overcooking? Bad digestion.

Probiotics are healthy bacteria in the gut that rid your intestines of bad stuff. The upshot? You're healthier when you get probiotics.

SEAWEEDS, which I like to think of as vegetables from the sea, include nori (used to wrap sushi), hijiki, wakame, dulse and many others. Extremely dense in minerals, they add a salty, oceanlike taste to dishes.

Asian establishments (in particular Japanese restaurants, as you can probably tell from the aforementioned names) serve seaweed often. So do vegetarian eateries. Not familiar with this food? Try a seaweed salad or ask for extra in your miso soup; both are easy, delicious ways to familiarize yourself with sea veggies—and to enjoy a big, healthy dose of minerals.

Feeling Fruity

Think of them as sweets that are good to eat: fruits are good sources of fiber, antioxidants, phytochemicals and vitamins, and provide energy via their easily digestible sugars.

They should comprise a small percentage of your overall plant intake, so it's appropriate that fruits make up a small percentage of the amount of plant food offered at restaurants—vegetables pop up all over menus, but fruits tend to appear only in juices, smoothies or desserts.

> **QUICK DEFINITION: CO-FACTOR**
>
> A co-factor is a nutrient that helps *another* nutrient work better.

And don't be concerned about creating huge spikes in blood sugar; it's generally not an issue because fruits come packaged with fiber and other co-factors. However, people with diabetes or who are prone to candida or yeast infections should go easy on sugary fruits like bananas or grapes, or avoid fruits altogether until their health problem is resolved. Here are details about fruits you're likely to find on Manhattan menus:

NON-SWEET FRUITS, such as peppers, tomatoes, and cucumbers, rank low on the glycemic index and therefore barely disrupt our blood-sugar balance. People with candida or diabetes can eat them safely. During the summer, I recommend checking out the many delicious varieties of locally grown heirloom tomatoes on offer.

FATTY FRUITS, such as avocadoes and olives, are arguably the best source of fats you can eat, because they are whole and come from plants (in contrast to many processed oils). Eaten raw, as they always should be, avocadoes and olives contain a fat-digesting enzyme, lipase, that makes them easy for our bodies to process. As a bonus, they're an excellent source of protein.

BERRIES are my favorite sweet fruits, both from a culinary perspective and nutritionally speaking. On the glycemic index, they rank lowest of all the sweet fruits, and, individually, each berry is touted for a specific attribute. For instance, blueberries offer a significant number of antioxidants, while raspberries help to nourish the female reproductive system.

In addition, several berries—especially goji berries and açai, the former a tart, bitter Tibetan berry, the latter the fruit of Amazonian palm trees—constitute a relatively new category of foods called superfruits, known as being exceptionally rich in nutrients. Sold in raw-food restaurants, goji berries in particular are also increasingly appearing in health-conscious eateries.

> **QUICK DEFINITION: GLYCEMIC INDEX**
>
> This system is a way of ranking a food's effect on your body's blood sugar, using the numbers one through 100. The lower the number, the better; foods assigned a high glycemic index cause rapid and unhealthy blood-sugar spikes.

CITRUS FRUITS include oranges, lemons, limes, and grapefruits. They tend to be high in immune-boosting vitamin C and in bioflavonoids—a type of antioxidant known for its anti-cancer properties, as well as its role in keeping blood capillaries healthy. Although citrus fruits taste acidic, they are, in fact, alkalizing and help to counteract the acidity of the meat, grains and beans that typically form the bulk of a restaurant meal.

ORCHARD FRUITS include apples, pears and peaches. Best eaten raw for their enzymes, soluble fiber and nutrients, these fruits usually show up in fruit salads and smoothies.

TROPICAL FRUITS like papayas, mangoes and pineapples are especially rich in the kinds of enzymes that are not only powerful aids to digestion, but also may help to break down scar tissue and waste materials in the body. Of course, being tropical, they're not local to New

York City. Nevertheless, they offer a tasty alternative to refined sugar for someone craving a sweet snack.

Grains and Bread

In many people's minds, grains—a fresh-baked loaf of bread, pasta with tomatoes and garlic—are a bit of an indulgence, okay when eaten here or there, but not to be devoured constantly. And, actually, I agree. If you tolerate them well, grains can add fiber, protein, other nutrients and enjoyment to your diet, as long as they're properly prepared, eaten in moderation, mostly in their whole form (I'll explain shortly) and organic (many grains are heavily sprayed and genetically modified).

That's not to say there aren't drawbacks. In fact, I specifically advise my clients to avoid the complimentary bread basket served before most meals. Why? The body treats grains—especially in the form of flour—like sugar, upsetting your blood-sugar balance and contributing to weight gain and insulin resistance. In addition, unless grains are soaked or sprouted, their bran layer will contain phytic acid, which reduces mineral absorption and enzyme inhibitors, which interfere with digestion. And, overall, grains cause the body to form mucus and are acidic; this last point means that the positive, alkaline effects of eating vegetables are partially neutralized when you eat grains.

So what is the best way to eat grains? Before I answer that, I should emphasize that not all grains are created equal, whether whole or refined. To address those differences, below I discuss the pros and cons of different grains. Overall, however, I recommend eating grains in their intact state (as opposed to milled grains like flour), such as brown rice, barley, oats, quinoa and—best of all—sprouted grains, made by soaking the grain in water until it germinates. Foods that aren't intact include those made from flour like breads, cakes and pasta as well as white rice. Brown rice is whole, but pasta made from brown-rice flour isn't—although it's preferable to wheat pasta.

QUICK DEFINITION: REFINED GRAINS

Refined grains are made by removing the bran (the outer layer) and the germ, which is rich in vitamin E. In the removal process, the fiber and most of the nutrients are lost. This is why brown rice is preferable to white. In addition, grains are further refined when they're milled into flour for breads and pasta.

A host of reasons underpin these recommendations. Flour is prone to rancidity. It causes a big, unhealthy spike in blood sugar (because the fiber, which has been removed, isn't there to slow down the release of carbs, which upset the body's blood-sugar balance when they're released too quickly). And refined grains like white rice and bread contain plenty of calories but little nutrition.

White wheat flour is one of the worst of the refined grains. In addition to having few nutrients and containing gluten, it's usually adulterated with bleaching agents and other chemicals to enhance its performance. Unfortunately, it's used in a whopping 90 percent of baked goods. Fortunately, there are some alternatives in addition to the whole grains just discussed.

Preparation techniques make a big difference; traditional methods yield more nutritious, easier-to-digest dishes. For example, the healthiest kind of bread you can order is the aforementioned sprouted grain bread, made from presoaked grains that are baked at low temperatures. Health-food restaurants often offer them. Sourdough bread is another smart choice, since it's naturally leavened with a traditional fermentation technique that neutralizes its phytic acid, increases its nutrients' availability and

> **TIP: AL DENTE PASTA**
>
> Al dente is the best option for cooked pasta because it only mildly affects your blood-sugar balance; overcooked pasta causes a rapid spike in blood sugar.

creates lactobacillus—friendly gut bacteria that aid digestion. And give dosas—a fermented, regional Indian grain product—a try. Made from rice and lentils that have been fermented for at least two days, dosas have a wonderful cheesy taste. Think of them as the south Indian equivalent of burritos—but more nutritious and easier to digest. My favorite choice for breads made directly from flour is spelt and whole rye.

Which brings me to a summary of my overall recommendations: Say yes to moderation, traditional preparation methods and whole grains—and no to refined, milled and non-organic versions. An overview of a selection of key grains follows. Although they all contain traces of gluten, I have divided them into gluten grains and non-gluten grains for people who are allergic. Even if you aren't, cutting down on gluten is good for your health.

GLUTEN GRAINS

WHEAT is the highest in gluten of all the grains, which is why it's the universal choice for bread making—gluten helps bread to rise. It's also the main ingredient in most pasta, pizza crusts, pastries, crackers, cakes, cookies and is even used as a thickener in sauces.

Given its ubiquity, wheat is not easy to avoid. That, plus the fact that it has addictive qualities, means that we tend to consume way too much of it. Nevertheless, I suggest making an effort to steer clear—or at least cut down—in part because wheat's high gluten level means it frequently disrupts the digestive system, even if you're not allergic. Reduce the percentage of wheat in your diet, and I suspect you'll be pleasantly surprised at how much better you feel day to day. (Incidentally, seitan—a popular meat substitute for vegetarians and vegans—is essentially wheat gluten with the texture of meat, so I recommend going easy on it.)

BULGUR AND COUSCOUS are actually wheat—tiny cracked pieces of it—and not a type of grain in their own right. Used like rice, bulgur is a staple in Middle Eastern restaurants and is best known as the main ingredient in tabbouleh. Couscous is typically found in North African or Moroccan cuisine.

KAMUT AND SPELT are non-hybridized, more ancient varieties of wheat. Because they're lower in gluten than wheat—and more nutritious to boot—both make good substitutes. In fact, you may do well on spelt even if you're sensitive to gluten, because the grain contains a different form of it. Fortunately, it's fairly easy to find spelt at health-conscious restaurants, where it's becoming increasingly popular as an ingredient for breads, baked goods and pizza crusts.

RYE, rich in a variety of nutrients, is used in place of wheat in items like rye bread and German pumpernickel. People who are mildly gluten sensitive tend to tolerate it in moderation. At restaurants, look for sandwiches made with whole rye.

BARLEY is one of the most ancient cultivated grains. Although it's supposed to be soothing to the intestines, it is also very acid-forming in the body.

OATS stabilize blood sugar, reduce cholesterol, and soothe the intestines and nervous system. Not usually encountered at dinner, they're most commonly served for breakfast as oatmeal or as a major component of granola and muesli. Oats also appear in some baked goods.

NON-GLUTEN GRAINS

RICE is the richest in B vitamins of all the grains and is served at all types of restaurants. It comes in numerous varieties: short-grain brown rice, which is central to the macrobiotic diet, is perhaps the most nutritious form, whereas white rice (especially the aromatic basmati) is more common than brown in Indian and Asian cuisine. Nowadays, though, most establishments offer a choice of brown or white. Brown is best; 70 percent of the nutrients and all of the fiber in white rice are lost in refining. In addition, steamed or boiled rice is preferable to fried; the latter contains damaged cooking oil.

CORN often comes from genetically modified crops, so always ask if it is organic. It turns up in restaurants as corn on the cob, as a side vegetable and in corn bread. Italian or upscale restaurants sometimes serve polenta, a mush of cornmeal usually offered as a side dish or appetizer.

BUCKWHEAT—usually in the form of the Russian staple kasha or in Japanese soba noodles—is one of a few commercial crops not routinely sprayed because it has its own natural resistance. With the longest transit time in the gut of all the grains, it is the most filling and stabilizing for blood sugar. And pre-roasting transforms buckwheat into one of the few alkalizing grains; kasha is essentially pre-roasted buckwheat.

QUINOA was a major grain for the Incas of South America. A relative newcomer to the restaurant scene, its mild taste and fluffy texture has made it enormously popular. And it's rich in high-quality protein, making it a favorite with vegetarians. If you're not familiar with quinoa, try it as an alternative to rice or oatmeal.

AMARANTH is currently not widely available in restaurants, but it is becoming increasingly popular. I recommend it to clients because it's very nutritious and contains many good amino acids such as lysine, which is low in several other grains.

MILLET, a cereal grass sometimes used in the U.S. as birdseed, but in all kinds of dishes in Asia and Africa, is another excellent option. It is alkaline, easily digested and very nutritious with a high silica content for healthy skin and bones.

Legumes

They're the punch line of bad jokes, true, but beans—as well as peas and lentils—confer many health benefits. Known as legumes, or pulses, they lower cholesterol, control blood-sugar imbalances and regulate bowel function. Low in fat (with the exception of soy beans), they're a good source of protein (especially for vegetarians and vegans), fiber and B vitamins. From a culinary perspective, herbs and spices marry well with the mild taste of legumes, which absorb the flavor of sauces and have a pleasant texture that adds bulk to any meal.

For a few susceptible individuals, abdominal gas and bloating result from eating beans, no matter how carefully they are prepared. But most of us need not avoid beans for fear of their antisocial effects. A good chef knows that most varieties of beans should be presoaked, rinsed and thoroughly cooked to break down their indigestible sugars and destroy their enzyme inhibitors (if they haven't come from a can). Here's the dish on beans:

Chickpeas, black beans, kidney beans, adzuki beans and lentils are among the legumes that crop up in numerous cultures where they have nourished humankind for millennia. For instance, chickpeas, also called garbanzo beans, are used to make the hummus and falafels of Mediterranean cuisine, as well as being popular in Indian curries; black beans are used in Mexican burritos; kidney beans are the legume of choice for chili; the adzuki bean is popular in macrobiotic restaurants; and red lentils often form the basis of dhal (dal, daal, dahl), an easily digested Indian puree.

SOY BEANS merit a lengthier discussion because they're eaten so frequently and used in so many ways—and, in particular, associated with numerous health claims and controversies.

Asians have been including soy foods in their diets for thousands of years, a fact that's often touted as the main reason for Asians' longevity and low rates of certain cancers and other Western diseases. However, this may have more to do with the paucity of dairy and meat in the Asian diet, as well as the emphasis on vegetables and various lifestyle factors. The truth is that soy has never been eaten in large quantities in Asia. Note the miso soup in Japanese restaurants, in which only a few cubes of tofu float around. And next time you order Chinese vegetables with soy-bean curd, observe how the vegetables and rice predominate. This marginal role for soy stands in stark contrast to the modern soy burger at the center of the vegetarian entrée.

Over the past few decades, vegetarians and vegans in particular have become overreliant on soy because it is a balanced protein and can be formed into mock meat. Restaurants dutifully offer soy, often in the form of tofu, as the vegetarian option for protein.

However, studies detailing soy's high nutrient content and positive effects have recently been contested by additional research. Worse, soy is known to block the absorption of some nutrients and is thought to increase the likelihood of ovarian and breast cancer. For more information, check out *The Whole Soy Story: The Dark Side of America's Favorite Health Food* by Dr. Kaayla Daniel; the book investigates the health problems linked to the overconsumption of soy.

One solution is simply to cut back. Another is to be mindful of the kinds of soy products you consume. Organic, non-GMO soy is your best bet, as are soy products like miso, soy yogurt, natto and tempeh, all of which undergo a fermentation process in which otherwise non-viable nutrients are partly predigested—and phytates and enzyme inhibitors that cause gastric distress are neutralized. In addition, those forms of soy are endowed with probiotics. With the possible exception of soy yogurt, these healthy forms of soy are usually available in Chinese, Japanese and macrobiotic restaurants.

Tofu, perhaps the most ubiquitous form of soy in restaurants, provides some nutrition but should be eaten in moderation since it hasn't undergone the all-important fermentation process. As for edamame, it's a whole food but not easy to digest—good for you, but not in excess, that is.

Soy milk, soy ice cream and soy cheese, however, are highly processed and not fermented—best consumed only on occasion. They usually come with additives of one kind or another, in an attempt to mimic the flavor and texture of the real thing.

Desserts made from hemp, almonds or rice are better choices. There's even an amazing raw, vegan ice cream made from cashews and sweetened with agave in New York State, available at organicnectars. com; persuade your neighborhood chef to place an order. Raw-food restaurants are likely to place this ice cream—or perhaps the chef's own creation—on the dessert menu.

A soy product that should be completely avoided whenever possible is textured vegetable (or soy) protein, also known as TVP, which in similar forms goes by the names protein soy isolate or hydrolyzed plant (or soy) protein. Made from soybean meal after the oil has been processed out with chemicals and intense pressure, TVP is used in veggie burgers and fake meats. TVP, soy isolate and hydrolyzed soy bear a close chemical resemblance to plastic and may contain residues from processing, including petroleum solvents, sulphuric acids, hydrochloric acid and caustic soda. Those are just a few good reasons to bypass that fake turkey sandwich in favor of the Tempeh Reuben.

MEAT STILL ENJOYS A reputation as being as all-American as the Wild West and cowboy boots. But improving yourself is an all-American quality, too, and to do that it's best to cut down on your intake of animal products, including fish, meat, poultry, dairy and eggs. I'm not saying that you have to become vegetarian or vegan, though; each individual should do what's best for his or her body.

THE FOURTH PRECEPT:

If you choose to eat animal products, consume only (a) high-quality and sustainably raised animals (ideally pasture-raised and grass-fed, but at least hormone and antibiotic-free); and do so (b) in moderation—meaning smaller portions with less frequency.

Remember how proponents of The China Study argue that meat-eating is a leading cause of human disease, but followers of the nutritionist Weston A. Price say that it can be beneficial? That's not the only area of contention regarding animal products. Another is over whether animal fats cause heart disease. An increasingly vocal minority of researchers claim that the cholesterol myth is just that—a myth. They believe that highly processed vegetable oils and hydrogenated fats are more artery-clogging and lead to more heart trouble than lard. Of course, adherents of veganism and vegetarianism eschew animal products for a variety of reasons, while others believe that those diets are lacking in some essential nutrients such as vitamins B12 and D.

Different people will side with different research; your genetic makeup or lifestyle may mean that eating meat is necessary for your body to function smoothly. To figure it out, I advocate experimenting and also thinking about how certain foods and dietary principles make you feel.

If you consume animal products, I hope that you do so in moderation. Why? Well, for one thing, animal products are higher in protein than necessary for human health, creating more acidity than the body can process and leading to problems like fatigue and osteoporosis. In addition, there's substantial evidence that the practice of raising animals for human consumption—especially in conventional corporate feedlots—is unsustainable and environmentally problematic. Easy ways to lower the percentage of animal products in your diet include thinking of meat as a side dish rather than a main course, as well as eating smaller portions less frequently.

In addition, make sure that all of the animal products you consume—beef, dairy, eggs, chicken and so on—come from high-quality, organic and pasture-fed animals. As well as having no fiber, animal products are a concentrated source of the medications, stress, hormones and environmental toxins that the animal has been exposed to. That's a powerful argument for choosing an organic, pasture-fed animal, which won't have been subjected to stressful conditions or injected with toxins like hormones and antibiotics. Instead, it will have been raised similarly to the way it would have been in the wild: a pasture-raised cow, for instance, grazes on grass, gets exercise and is exposed to the sun, all of which results in a healthy cow—and extra benefits for us.

REMINDER: DON'T NECESSARILY WORRY ABOUT ORGANIC CERTIFICATION

Small farmers who raise animals sustainably and hormone- and antibiotic-free often can't afford to obtain the accreditation "certified organic."

To summarize: make sure that the animal products you eat are high quality and organic (that is, hormone- and antibiotic-free) and preferably grass-fed. In addition, consume them less often and in small portions—and eat them with vegetables (especially leafy greens) to counteract some of the potential negative effects. By making those tweaks, you ensure that high-quality meat, fish, poultry, dairy and eggs can become a healthy part of a balanced diet rather than a risk factor. In the following two sections, I round up the different kinds of animal foods appearing on restaurant menus.

Meat and Fish

Not all meats are created equal. Some are organic, some not; some grilled, others fried. Part of the purpose of this section is to further clarify and help you choose the healthiest options.

For instance, grilled or roasted meats are better for you than deep-fried dishes. Be aware, though, that meats smoked or barbecued on charcoal grills can develop a carcinogen called polycyclic aromatic hydrocarbons. Like most other foods, meat is best for your body when it has been cooked briefly and gently. Prolonged high heat reduces the amount of vitamins and minerals in meat and denatures its protein. Worse, it increases the toxicity of contaminants already there, such as nitrates and pesticides. Of course, with the disease-causing pathogens showing up in animal products, it may not be such a bad idea to avoid rare or raw meat (which otherwise would be the healthiest way to consume high-quality, properly raised animal products). However, when possible, ask that your meat not be overcooked. Medium-rare is a good option and usually what chefs prefer anyway.

Here are details about the different types of meats you're likely to encounter on menus:

BEEF is a source of iron and vitamin B12, as well as essential fats. Cows raised in pastures—where they're exposed to the sun and eat grass—provide the healthiest meat; in fact, an essential fat and anti-cancer nutrient called conjugated linoleic acid (CLA) occurs only in grass-fed animals.

One rung down from grass-fed cows is organic beef, which means that the animal has been raised without hormones and antibiotics, but has been fed grains, corn or organic vegetarian feed. Often this is for taste reasons but sometimes even these animals are overfed in an attempt to fatten them up, a practice that makes them more prone to disease. Since grass is the natural diet for cows, animals that eat grains or corn—even if it's high-quality organic—are not as healthy as their grass-fed counterparts and therefore not as healthy for humans.

And as far as factory-farmed beef goes, I advise avoiding it altogether because of the health, environmental and moral issues involved. Jammed together in pens where they never see sunlight and are injected with hormones and who knows what else, the cows raised in such farms are usually very sick—part of the reason they're injected with excess antibiotics. That's an excellent reason to opt for grass-fed, sustainably raised beef—or, at the very least, a hormone and antibiotic-free animal.

And think of the fact that it may be a tad pricey as a motivator for you to eat less meat overall; as you may recall, I'm a big proponent of eating meat in moderation.

CHICKEN, LAMB and **PORK**, all sources of protein, can be good for you, like beef, if you choose an organic, naturally raised animal and eat it in moderation.

When it comes to pork, though, don't be fooled by the advertising ("The New White Meat"). It's actually probably less healthy for you than chicken or lamb. And it makes such a difference to your health that I'll say it again: order free-range, naturally fed chicken, lamb or pork—and consume small portions.

GAME ANIMALS like boar and venison are among the healthiest kinds of meats because they come from freshly killed animals that lived in the wild. These animals are leaner than beef or chicken and boast a higher proportion of omega-3 fatty acids. In addition, they're less likely to be contaminated or diseased. It is becoming easier to find boar and venison in trendy restaurants, as well as establishments emphasizing organic dishes, although, for some, venison's gamey flavor is an acquired taste.

CURED MEATS like sausages, luncheon meats and bacon can be okay to eat in moderation; it all comes down to how they are raised and made. I recommend cutting out luncheon meats altogether—nearly all of them contain carcinogenic preservatives such as nitrates. If you can't stay away from, say, bologna, at least get a package labeled "nitrate-free." Two requirements should be met before you purchase bacon or sausage: (1) The meat should have come from a good-quality animal, one that was naturally raised and fed (hormone- and antibiotic-free). (2) The way the meat was made should be as natural as possible. Sausage without casings or fillers, produced on the premises at an organic restaurant, for instance, gets my thumbs-up—as long as you eat it in moderation.

FOIE GRAS and **VEAL** tend to be served only in upscale restaurants; the former is the liver of a fattened-up goose or duck, and the latter is the meat of a milk-fed (or sometimes formula-fed) baby calf.

A lot of people avoid veal and foie gras (French for "fat liver") for moral reasons. Since I don't see any particular health benefits from eating either of these foods, I recommend avoiding them altogether.

COLD-WATER FISH like salmon, mackerel, cod and sardines, are chock-full of heart-healthy omega 3 fatty acids as well as fat-soluble vitamins and minerals, including iodine. Unfortunately, these goodies are meaningless if the fish is conventionally farm-raised, a technique that results in more PCBs, mercury and disease—and fewer omega 3's. Plus, the feed for farmed salmon usually contains dye to give the flesh a pink color.

If you want the benefits of organically farm-raised or wild fish, salmon—a potent source of omega 3—is probably the easiest fish to find at restaurants. Most nutritious in its raw form (for instance, as sushi), it's also healthy when steamed or baked. Skip tempura, though; it involves dipping fish in batter before deep-frying it in hot oil.

SCAVENGER FISH include tuna, swordfish, carp and catfish. They eat almost anything they find in the sea, including already-dead fish (yum!). That's why their tissues are likely to contain the toxins of other fish, like PCBs and mercury; it's also why scavenger fish are considered no-no's for women who are pregnant or breastfeeding. If you like fish, I suggest sticking mostly to the cold-water kind.

SHELLFISH is a category that includes scallops, clams, mussels, oysters, shrimp, crabs and lobsters. They should be eaten in moderation and always while very fresh and in season. For a number of reasons, I am not a huge fan. Shellfish spoil easily and are a common cause of food

> **INTERESTING TIDBIT: ORGAN MEATS**
>
> A few nutritionally-minded types, including followers of Weston A. Price, believe that the healthiest part of an animal to eat is its organs, like the liver—as long as it comes from a properly-raised animal (when we consume meat, we tend to eat steak, which is a muscle).

poisoning, as well as being prone to contamination. Be sure yours are sourced from clean waters.

To help you make quality seafood choices when you're shopping or out to eat, download the *Seafood Pocket Guide* at (http://edf.org/documents/1980_pocket_seafood_selector.pdf). It lists fish both high in omega-3 fats and low in environmental contaminants.

Dairy and Eggs

Cheese conjures up sophisticated images like wine-and-cheese parties, while milk perhaps sounds quaint (think milkmen in the 1950s). Like those varying images, dairy and eggs have varying effects on your health, depending on who you are, how much you eat and the quality of what you consume. Frankly, I'm not the biggest advocate of consuming a lot of dairy, but I try to stay open-minded.

Dairy's big selling point is that it's a source of calcium. Yet milk's acidity means that it actually leaches calcium from the bones. In addition, its low magnesium content in relation to its calcium (they are required in balance for proper utilization) means that the calcium may not get completely used by the body. It's better obtained from vegetables, seeds and nuts.

Another reason I'm not a big fan of dairy products is their tendency to create mucus in the body, resulting in anything from a runny nose to a clogged-up digestive system.

In addition, many people are lactose intolerant; only around a third of the world's population possesses the genetic mutation required for the proper digestion of dairy. Asian and African-American populations include an especially high percentage of milk-intolerant individuals, which is why you're not likely to find many dairy products on the menu at an Asian restaurant.

That doesn't mean dairy is the devil, at least not for people who digest it well—as long as you get it from grass-fed cows, or at minimum, opt for an organic version. I recommend avoiding products containing Recombinant Bovine Growth Hormone, aka RBGH, a genetically engineered drug associated with growth abnormalities and malignant tumors. Another reason to go organic: dairy cows fed unnatural diets, forced to produce excessive quantities of milk, confined to small stalls or kept in unhygienic conditions often suffer from infected udders. This infection, called mastitis, causes the sick cows to release pus into their milk.

A roundup of dairy products commonly found in restaurants follows.

MILK itself doesn't feature prominently on most menus, but it crops up in sauces, smoothies and as a side dish for tea and coffee. Even so, cow's milk contains more protein than we need and can cause weight gain. Some organic-focused restaurants offer preferable alternatives like rice, almond or hemp milk (note that I didn't include soy, which I addressed earlier); ask the staff if you don't see any of those options on the menu.

CHEESE is often a concentrated form of milk, best eaten in moderation. Some of my clients who want to reduce their cheese consumption find it extremely hard to do so; cheese is considered one of the most difficult foods to stop eating (in addition to sugar) because of its casein, a protein with addictive qualities.

One partial solution is to eat better types of cheese, like raw (unpasteurized) versions, which retain more enzymes and nutrients, and boast an arguably better taste than their pasteurized counterparts. Although they're not yet common in the United States, with demand, their availability is increasing, particularly in restaurants that stress organic or specialty foods.

Sheep and goat cheeses are another smart alternative. Easier to digest than cheese made from cow's milk, these cheeses are increasingly popular in restaurants, where you might find them atop salads and as sandwich fillings.

And no surprise here: I recommend avoiding processed cheese, a staple in some sandwiches and fast-food entrées; they usually contain additives such as emulsifiers, extenders, phosphates and hydrogenated oils. You'll likely find them easy to give up, considering their bland taste and plastic texture.

CULTURED DAIRY PRODUCTS—kefir, yogurt and sour cream—are easier to digest than other dairy items because their lactose and casein are already partially broken down. Kefir is a liquid yogurt traditionally created from camel's milk, although many versions use cow's milk. Most Greek and Indian restaurants serve yogurt; the latter may also use ghee in food preparation. Well tolerated by most people, ghee is butter with the milk solids removed.

BUTTER most often appears at your table accompanying a complimentary basket of bread. Unless you have a dairy allergy, a moderate amount of butter—especially organic—offers some benefits, including easily digested fats and the fat-soluble vitamins A and D.

ICE CREAM and **CREAM** populate the dessert section of many menus. Practice moderation, or try some of the naturally sweetened nut-based ice creams popping up at raw-food restaurants.

EGGS are often classified with dairy products (especially by vegetarians) because, like milk and cheese, they come from animals but the animals don't have to be killed to obtain the food. Rich in vitamins, minerals and protein, eggs can be quite nourishing.

> **TIP:**
> **EAT THE WHOLE EGG**
>
> Egg whites contain an enzyme inhibitor that's neutralized by the yolk. So don't eat only the whites—eat the whole shebang, yolk and whites. Your digestion will thank you.

Their cholesterol content causes debate, however; overcooked, it becomes oxidized, meaning it transforms from a useful nutrient into a potentially harmful chemical. For that reason (i.e., they contain oxidized cholesterol), avoid powdered eggs, which have been through a heating and drying process. To avoid oxidation in your egg order, ask for lightly poached or sunny-side-up eggs rather than scrambled or fried; similarly, soft-boiled trumps hard-boiled. Raw eggs are even more beneficial than the lightly cooked kind. However, people susceptible to salmonella, such as the elderly, the infirm or pregnant women, should avoid raw eggs.

As with dairy and meat, a chef's choice of egg supplier has implications for both nutritional quality and taste. Battery-caged hens tend to turn out eggs with salmonella, few nutrients and a bland or fishy taste—and the cruelty of crowding hens together is another reason to skip ordering such eggs. Free-range, pasture-raised hens, on the other hand, produce unpredictable eggs; as with heirloom vegetables, the result is a richer flavor and increased nutrient content. At the very least, stick with hormone- and antibiotic-free eggs taken from cage-free hens.

IN THE NEXT SECTION, I discuss the kinds of things that make your mouth water—sweeteners, seasonings, fats and oils, and beverages. These more subtle foods may be potentially harmful, but they don't have to be, as long as you approach these full-of-flavor foods the right way. Which brings me to my final premise, one that by now you know, but which I'd like to highlight once more.

THE FIFTH PRECEPT: To feel better immediately, simply reduce your intake of artificial, chemical-laden processed foods as well as sugar, caffeine and alcohol.

As you read through the next few categories, keep this precept in mind. It's actually less difficult to follow than you might think; stick to the natural flavorings, not the substances created in a test tube. Do those long, chemical, hard-to-pronounce names even sound that tasty? Not really, right? Educating yourself about all of the tasty *and* natural substances out there (honey, anyone?) is the perfect insurance against being lured away by processed foods.

Fats and Oils
They've got a less-than-savory rep, but don't be afraid of fats and oils. They play an important role in the human diet.

Fats and oils slow the release of sugar from other foods, create a feeling of satisfaction, give us a source of energy and allow us to absorb fat-soluble vitamins, including A, D, E and K by carrying them across the gut wall. In addition, our bodies use fats as building materials, incorporating them into the cell membranes to create the right balance between firmness and flexibility.

We like to preach about its evils—weight gain, heart disease—while still associating fatty food with comfort and fun. Truth is, it can get kind of complicated, so let's simplify. The list of different fats and oils is a long one, so here's what you need to know about the ones you are most likely to encounter at a restaurant.

Trans fats or hydrogenated oils, made by injecting hydrogen into liquid vegetable oils to make them more solid, should be completely avoided as they are probably the most harmful ingredient in our food supply. In fact, New York City has ensured you'll avoid these oils because in 2008, the city banned the use of trans fats in restaurants. So it is far less likely than before that dining out will mean consuming damaged vegetable oils in the form of vegetable shortening and hydrogenated margarine.

Avocadoes, raw nuts and seeds, coconuts and olives should form the bulk of your fat intake and are excellent sources of essential fatty acids, fiber and other co-factors (when these foods are turned into oils, some of these goodies are eliminated). These plant fats should not cause weight gain as part of a balanced diet, nor should they contribute to heart disease.

Whole coconut meat is preferable to coconut oil or coconut butter, although those latter two don't deserve the artery-blocking image painted by some, even though they are a saturated fat. Want to learn more? Take a look at *The Healing Properties of Coconut Oil* by nutritionist Bruce Fife.

HEMP SEEDS and FLAXSEEDS are valued for their essential fatty acids, but they are best used whole and raw since processing, storage and heating can turn these delicate oils rancid. Flax contains more omega 3 than fish (minus contaminants such as mercury and PCBs), but you can't cook with flax oil—it's best to eat the seeds. Hemp and flax oils are healthy only when cold-pressed; in that form, they make an excellent salad dressing.

OLIVE OIL is a monounsaturated fat. Even though it has negligible amounts of essential fatty acids, it's better than many other oils and doesn't contain a high amount of harmful omega 6. And the form in which it's served at most quality restaurants—as salad dressing—is good, since it has more benefits when raw, especially if it's extra virgin, organic and cold-pressed. It crops up in that form at Italian and Mediterranean establishments. Like most oils, though, olive oil is damaged by high heat.

BUTTER has become cool again after the downfall of margarine because of its dangerous levels of trans fat (hydrogenated oils). I believe butter—especially organic butter from a grass-fed cow—has some health benefits when consumed in moderation. Margarine, on the other hand, can damage your arteries more than any amount of butterfat because of its aforementioned trans fats. Its overuse in recent years—along with oils like soy, sunflower and corn—has contributed to a national over-consumption of omega 6 fats versus omega 3, a situation that has been linked to numerous health problems.

Salt and Seasonings

My friends like to tease that I have a "salt tooth" in contrast to most people's "sweet tooth," but I've learned to treat salt as I would sugar—with fondness but also caution.

Salt provides sodium, an important mineral involved in many bodily processes. However, it's unhealthy when you're getting a lot of sodium but hardly any potassium, a mineral found mainly in fresh fruits and vegetables. That's because sodium and potassium work together as intimate partners. It is essential that they remain in proper balance for the smooth functioning of our muscles, lungs, heart and nervous system, as well as for the water balance within our bodies. In particular, many people suffer from raised blood pressure, muscle cramps and water retention when they consume too much salt.

Most people get *way* more than enough salt whether they try to or not, just because salt, and therefore sodium, is overabundant in our modern, processed meals. Potassium, however, is lacking, because we don't eat enough vegetables. We need less than half a teaspoon of sodium per day, but many of us are consuming *seven* times that amount.

At a restaurant, you can request that your meal be prepared with less salt. You'll be amazed at how quickly you lose the desire for excess salt and start to find too much unappealing—I certainly have, despite my "salt tooth."

TIP: GOOD SALT SUBSTITUTES

One clever and healthful way to reduce your sodium intake at a restaurant is to ask for extra garlic, ginger, herbs or spices to be substituted instead, a move that will increase the flavor of your meal while adding some health benefits. Some of the best additions are garlic, a natural antibiotic; ginger, an anti-inflammatory and digestive aid; cayenne, a circulation enhancer; turmeric, an antioxidant and anti-inflammatory; and green herbs such as parsley or cilantro, a good source of vitamins and chlorophyll.

REFINED TABLE SALT tends to be processed and altered with chemicals—it's sodium chloride with no nutritional benefits. I recommend deleting it from your diet, since it contributes to the sodium-potassium imbalance described above and usually contains aluminum to boot.

KOSHER SALT is a coarse salt with no additives; its thick crystal grains help to cure meat, thus its name (since it's used by some Jews to make meat kosher). Foodies like this salt for its texture and taste; perhaps because it appears in gourmet foods, it's sometimes thought to be healthier than table salt. That's not the case, however; there's no nutritional difference between table and kosher salt (the latter may be marginally more healthful because it doesn't have additives, but don't be fooled into thinking it's good for you).

SEA SALT or **HIMALAYAN CRYSTAL SALT** both appear at some restaurants and are fine to eat in moderation. Natural and unprocessed, they contain minerals from the ocean, have a better flavor than table salt and tend to be prized by good chefs. Although sea and crystal salt are gaining in popularity, they're still currently most likely to crop up in the kitchens of health-food or gourmet restaurants. At raw-food restaurants, they're usually the only kind of salt offered.

BRAGG'S LIQUID AMINOS is a low-sodium alternative to soy sauce (although it's made from soy beans) that appears on the tables of many health-food restaurants. Although it's better than table salt, I tend not to think of it as a health food. Despite its name, the amount of amino acids (i.e., protein) that it provides is negligible. And like soy sauce, it has been found to contain some naturally occurring monosodium glutamate (MSG), a flavor-enhancer that has been associated with various health problems. Nevertheless, it does add a strong, savory flavor to meals.

SHOYU and **TAMARI**, both commonly referred to as soy sauce, are more or less interchangeable; both are fermented soy condiments, except that tamari is wheat-free. Asian and health-food restaurants serve shoyu and tamari, where they're sometimes also used for stir-frying. Health conscious diners prefer naturally brewed versions over highly processed and additive-laden cheaper imitations. However, I find soy sauce a questionable substitute for table salt because of the soy, wheat and the inevitable processing. Unless stated on the label, soy sauce is not a low-sodium alternative and is best used sparingly.

Sweeteners

"You're sweet." "How sweet it is." "That's *sweet*." The English language is peppered with instances of how, well, *sweet* sweetness is. So it's understandable that sugary foods are where I get the most resistance and guilt from my clients.

It's not exactly a news flash that refined white sugar and the more insidious high fructose corn syrup is bad for us. It's difficult to get away from, though, because sugar is in all kinds of foods—not just bottled drinks and desserts, but also savory sauces.

Even if we're aware of which foods contain refined white sugar, it's hard not to order them anyway. That's because sugar is addictive. Stop eating it and you'll experience withdrawal symptoms. Eat some and you will crave more. Sounds like an addiction to me. Then there's the emotional aspect of sugar cravings. Consider how children are offered sweets if they're "good" or "behave." To make matters worse, it seems that we have been biologically programmed to seek out sweetness as a way to avoid poison, which tends to be bitter. But I bet evolution intended for us to eat fruits and not, say, doughnuts.

Even though you know that sweets are bad for you, it's worth pointing out the many ways they're bad. Sugar is an anti-nutrient, not only giving the body zero nutrition, but actually robbing us of goodies. Plus, it's probably the major contributor to weight gain; at a certain point of saturation, the body converts it to fat, putting excess sugar into storage in order to quickly remove it from the blood where it would otherwise create havoc. After all, there is only so much sugar that we can use as energy. Sugar has been linked to a variety of other ailments, from lowered immunity and poor gut flora to cancer and diabetes.

Yet, according to the USDA, we are eating increasingly more sugar. The average American consumes over a cup a day of the stuff—an increase of 23 percent between 1985 and 1999.

So what should we do? Well, we have to be really smart about our approach. Something I have noticed with my clients is that once they begin to take better care of themselves in other areas of their lives and eat better-quality foods, their cravings tend to lessen. Sometimes exercise helps, as does eating a little more protein and drinking more water. I always suggest a switch to more natural, gentler forms of sweeteners. Take these steps and over time you will gradually experience refined sugar as being too sweet and tasting fake. True, it may take a while, but I've found that this approach has worked, not only for me but for many former sugar addicts with whom I've worked.

Let's take a look at some of the common sweeteners you will encounter at restaurants.

WHITE TABLE SUGAR, HIGH FRUCTOSE CORN SYRUP and even **BROWN SUGAR** should be avoided as much as possible.

ORGANIC RAW CANE SUGAR, FLORIDA CRYSTALS and **TURBINADO SUGAR** have gained in popularity and are commonly found on the tables and in desserts at health-food restaurants. Although I am not a big fan and don't use them myself, I believe they are a slightly better option than the completely refined stuff, since these kinds of sugars do retain some nutrients and are better for the environment. But they're not healthy.

MAPLE SYRUP and **BROWN RICE SYRUP** are preferable to all of the above. They are the most commonly consumed natural sweeteners. While not ideal because they can negatively impact existing digestive issues and have a fairly high glycemic index, they are okay in moderation if they are pure and of a high quality.

HONEY is a far better choice than many of the other sweeteners, especially the raw, unheated varieties, which are rich in antioxidants, enzymes and various healing co-factors.

RAW AGAVE NECTAR has fast become the sweetener of choice among those looking to avoid refined sugar. I believe it's a better option than refined sugar, yet it still has its issues, including a very high fructose content and production quality. I suggest using it in moderation.

STEVIA (technically a supplement), extracted from the sweet leaves of the stevia plant, is also becoming increasingly popular for its highly sugary taste and safeness for diabetics, although some people are not crazy about its aftertaste. In addition, although it has been used safely by humans for a long time, there is conflicting research in regard to its safety.

More and more restaurants are providing agave and stevia for tea or coffee, as well as using them in place of sugar in desserts and baked goods.

ARTIFICIAL SWEETENERS like Splenda, Equal or NutraSweet (aspartame) should be avoided. There are more adverse reactions to NutraSweet reported to the FDA than to all other foods and additives combined. Plus, there is even convincing evidence that these artificial sweeteners lead to weight gain.

Beverages

A sparkling stream of water runs through a picturesque valley. This could be an ad for anything from beer to an energy drink. The point? Advertisers know that we know that water is good for us. So they use it to sell beverages that aren't so good. Read on for details about the drinks you'll find at restaurants.

WATER should be your beverage of choice, in my opinion; usually it's the most natural and purest liquid you can get. Bottled water in restaurants tends to be overpriced, but it may be worth it if the only other option is unfiltered tap water, which will be polluted by chlorine and fluoride, among other contaminants. Filtered tap water is the best option; it's free, safe and better for the environment than bottled water (plus, you avoid ingesting chemicals that may leach into the water from the plastic bottle). If the restaurant's water is filtered, the food that's cooked in it will be safer for you as well.

> **TIP: WATER TEMPERATURE**
>
> Room-temperature water is the healthiest kind. That's because ice-cold water is difficult to digest, so ask for yours with no ice—but with a slice of lemon, which makes the water more alkalizing and cleansing.

FRUIT JUICES are okay to drink but quite sugary, which is why I recommend diluting them with water. **VEGETABLE JUICES**: much better. They count toward your nutrient intake, especially with dark greens thrown in.

SODAS and **SOFT DRINKS** are composed of unfiltered, artificially carbonated water with added sugar (or, worse, corn syrup or artificial sweeteners), flavorings, colorings, preservatives and sometimes caffeine. In addition, their high phosphoric-acid content is associated with osteoporosis. Not a recipe for health. I recommend avoiding them altogether, especially the diet ones, which are loaded with artificial sweeteners that, research has suggested, actually may cause weight gain.

As long as they're sweetened with fruit juice instead of cane sugar, natural sodas are fine to drink in moderation, since they're made from cleaner water and are caffeine-free.

TIP: ELECTROLYTES FOR ATHLETES

Looking to replenish those electrolytes after a tough workout? Replace your Gatorade with coconut water. It's loaded with electrolytes and a naturally sweet taste to boot.

COFFEE, provided by most restaurants, can provide a much-needed lift. Still, my recommendation is to reduce caffeine consumption with the goal of eventually giving it up altogether. Sure, coffee beans may contain antioxidants; plus, some people metabolize caffeine better than others. However, caffeine in general, and coffee in particular, is linked to raised blood pressure, insomnia, nervous conditions, osteoporosis and certain cancers. At the very least, imbibing caffeine with your meal reduces the availability of minerals in the food—it leaches them out.

If you can't resist ordering a cup, check whether the restaurant offers an organic, fair-trade or shade-grown version.

GREEN TEA may be the most healthful, or at least the most benign, of all caffeinated beverages. That's because it contains polyphenols, a type of antioxidant that can reduce blood pressure (note coffee's opposite effect), lower blood fats and combat those free radicals we encounter in a city environment. It contains much less caffeine than coffee. In addition, it has theanine, which mitigates some of caffeine's effects to produce a calmer type of energy and prevents a caffeine "hangover."

TIP: COFFEE REPLACEMENT

• Raw cacao beans, or nibs, make a tasty interim crutch for people trying to break their coffee habit. Cacao will give you a lift—partially from caffeine, and partially from other natural happiness-inducing chemicals. Plus, it's extraordinarily rich in magnesium and antioxidants (sorry, chocolate bars with their cooked cacao and sugar don't count as a whole-food alternative to coffee). Restaurants that serve raw or live desserts—meaning enzymes and healthy bacteria are active in the food—often offer a raw cacao fix, sweetened with agave nectar to boot.
• Green tea, which contains less caffeine than coffee and has energy-giving theanine, offers a healthful boost.
• Grain coffee substitutes, especially popular in macrobiotic restaurants, are caffeine-free yet have coffee's robust taste.

BLACK TEA has fewer antioxidants and more caffeine than green. But it doesn't contain as much caffeine as coffee, unless it is steeped for an especially long time.

Both green and black tea come from the same plant, often one that's been heavily sprayed, so seek out an organic version.

DECAFFEINATED TEA or **COFFEE** is fine to drink if the caffeine has been removed using the Swiss-water process. Otherwise, residue from chemicals used to remove the caffeine might remain—a non-issue if the product is certified organic. And note that all decaffeinated beverages still contain some traces of caffeine.

HERBAL TEAS may be the best hot drink overall, since they are naturally caffeine-free and boast mild therapeutic benefits. For instance, peppermint and ginger tea both are helpful to drink after a heavy meal, since they aid digestion; chamomile, as you probably know, has calming properties.

FERMENTED DRINKS are digestive aids, rich in enzymes and probiotics. They tend to be offered by establishments that focus on traditional health foods. Kombucha tea is not technically a tea, but rather a fermented cold drink made by steeping a mushroomlike growth in water. Rich in enzymes, probiotics and B vitamins, kombucha is a wonderful aid to digestion and general well-being. A "live" product, this tea is popular in raw- and health-food restaurants. Other common kinds of fermented drinks include amazake, made from rice; kefir, which is lacto-fermented milk; and ginger ale and apple cider, both healthy when made using old-fashioned methods.

WINE is fermented, true, but I believe that its alcohol content tends to neutralize the much-touted health benefits. Although wine has been in the news as being good for you in various small ways, my experience is that people use that as an excuse to drink too much. Even in relatively small amounts, wine is an anti-nutrient, particularly good at robbing the body of B vitamins. All alcohol can make you accident prone, dehydrated, unable to concentrate and even aggressive. It should be avoided if you are susceptible to candida overgrowth. And it's worth repeating: long-term drinking to excess, whether labeled alcoholism or not, can result in liver damage and stomach ulcers, not to mention a host of social and emotional problems.

Still, like coffee, alcohol can be useful in moderation. After a stressful day at work, a relaxing glass of wine can make all the difference to your enjoyment of a meal and your ability to converse with fellow diners. Plus, it can stimulate the digestive process. Red wine in particular provides some antioxidant benefits and is said to be good for the heart in moderate amounts. As with coffee, though, there is no need to rely on wine for your antioxidants; think vegetables and fruits instead.

If you do choose to consume alcohol, organic beer or red wine is the best choice; like other organic goods, these drinks should be free of pesticides. And biodynamic wine is arguably better than regular organic, since biodynamic producers go to extraordinary lengths to create special, pure growing conditions.

Restaurants with an extensive wine list may offer one labeled sulphite-free or NSA, meaning "no sulphites added." Sulphites occur naturally on grapes, but many vineyards add more to prevent bacterial growth, oxidation and a vinegary taste. Many people experience allergic side effects, including headaches, when they consume sulphites, and some connoisseurs prefer the taste of a low-sulphite wine. White wine generally has fewer sulphites than red.

BEER, ALE and **LAGER** are lower in alcohol than wine, but it's still important to watch the amount that you drink.

HARD LIQUOR or **SPIRITS** such as vodka, tequila, or rum are much higher in alcohol than both wine and beer, which is why they're often diluted with tonic water or fruit juice. Be especially careful of these because of the high alcohol content.

MAKING IT ALL WORK

I'M NOT THE KIND of guy to just hand you the facts and run. What do you do now that I've provided an education about different foods? Well, first let's remind ourselves what those *Five Precepts* are:

1 There's more than one right way to eat.
2 The overwhelming majority of your diet should consist of natural, high-quality and whole foods.
3 Everyone would be better off if a larger proportion of their diet consisted of plants—mostly vegetables (in particular, leafy greens), and some nuts, seeds and fruits.
4 If you choose to eat animal products, consume only (a) high-quality and sustainably raised animals (ideally pasture-raised and grass-fed, but at least hormone and antibiotic-free); and do so (b) in moderation—meaning smaller portions with less frequency.
5 To feel better immediately, simply reduce your intake of artificial, chemical-laden processed foods as well as sugar, caffeine and alcohol.

I want to make it easy for you to transition—and stick—to healthier dining, so here are several psychological and social tips for following the precepts outlined above.

The Right Approach
MOTIVATION

This is the *why*: You've got to know why you're doing something to be able to really carry it out.

So, why are you changing your diet? Okay, I confess. We all, including me, want to be slimmer, trimmer, better looking. And those are okay reasons. But there are better reasons, like heightened energy, greater strength, fewer illnesses and clearer thinking. I find that it helps to get excited about getting the most out of life and bringing enjoyment not only to yourself, but also to other people—not to mention planet earth— since our food choices have a major impact on the environment.

So, right now, take out a sheet of paper and write down *why* you want to eat healthier. Once you've written down your motivations, commit to them—that is, setting a clear intention. It's a great launching pad for getting—and staying—motivated.

The other part of intention and motivation? Believing that, yes, you can do this. Don't simply hope you can succeed; know that you will.

AWARENESS

Awareness means (a) remembering your motivation (your *why*) and intention (your commitment); and (b) being aware of the various forces that might act against you. Admitting that challenges exist is a necessary step to moving beyond them.

These challenges include: physical cravings and addictions, emotional attachments to food, cultural conditioning, advertising and a lack of education about healthy eating. Peer pressure is another biggie; you're going to need to keep your resolve if others try to coax you back to your old ways. Just be aware that change can make others uncomfortable.

Realize that these scenarios are not personal to you. They are issues for all of us, since we are all human and ever-evolving. Therefore, be aware that you are not a victim.

Awareness also means paying attention to how certain foods make us feel, physically and mentally. Keep a diet diary if that helps. Begin to eliminate any foods or drinks that drain your energy, give you indigestion, make you irritable or create so much guilt when you consume them that you simply don't enjoy or digest them properly.

PATIENCE

Do you wish I had a magic formula for positive change? Actually, I do. Think of it as the magical trio: patience, perseverance and resilience. Okay, I admit it: those qualities aren't so simple.

In dietary terms, those words mean realizing that lasting improvements take time and application. At first you may need to be satisfied with eating healthier about half of the time, but once you do get to that 50/50 mark, you will have the momentum to go further, slowly, going from 60/40 to 70/30 and onward, until you may even hit 90/10. Don't be too extreme right away, though. Just start with the 50 percent rule and see what happens. En route, don't be discouraged by slip-ups. Just notice it and move on.

> **YOUR CHOICES AS AN INDIVIDUAL**
>
> Part of being human is having the ability to make conscious choices based on our intentions and what is best for us.

After a while, you'll notice that, bit by bit, you're starting to find excess sugar and salt unpalatable. In the meantime, instead of dwelling on what you need to eliminate, simply eat more of the good stuff so that it crowds out both the desire and the space for unhealthy foods.

Try not to be too rigid with yourself or others. People who are hard on themselves tend to be judgmental of others. That's counterproductive. If your mission to eat better becomes a strict chore and strains your relationships, it will make you miserable and longing for your old, comfortable ways. Remember what works for your body may not necessarily work for someone else's; that's bio-individuality.

How to Eat

Of course, I couldn't possibly lay down the rules of such a personal and elusive concept as "how to eat." Nevertheless, here are some helpful tips:

STAY NOURISHED: Stay on top of cravings by beginning the day with a sustaining breakfast and eating a nutritious lunch. Make lunch your largest meal of the day, and when possible eat dinner early and fairly light—a large salad or vegetarian option, for instance—so that you're not overeating close to bedtime. And keep hydrated all day by drinking water.

CHEW: Sounds obvious, but you'd be surprised how many people don't, at least not properly. Thorough mastication helps your body digest nutrients better. To see just how little chewing we all do, try chewing 10 to 20 times per mouthful or until the food becomes liquid—not easy, right?

EAT SLOWLY: Pause between bites to savor the flavors and check in with your stomach to ask it "are you full yet?" This will make your meal last longer and help to prevent the discomfort and weight gain associated with overeating.

DON'T OVEREAT: Eating slowly and chewing properly helps to prevent this, but note how much you order in the first place. Practice portion control. And realize that it's unnecessary to order an appetizer and dessert as well as an entrée. If you're still hungry after eating slowly, you can always order more. Have a light fruit snack before going out to eat; if you arrive at a restaurant starving, you're likely to overeat. And skip the bread at the beginning of the meal.

AVOID DISTRACTIONS: If you're not good at blocking out extraneous noise and distractions, you might want to eat in silence or alone occasionally. But given that most meals—especially in restaurants—

are a fun, shared experience, try to dine with people who don't give you indigestion. Keep heated debates to a minimum so that you can chew and assimilate the food properly. Reading and television are also distracting.

DON'T EAT UNDER STRESS: Anxiety and anger shut down the digestive function as part of the "fight or flight" response. Eating under such circumstances can cause indigestion. At such times you will be tempted to go for comfort foods or to overeat to numb your feelings. If you do arrive stressed at a restaurant, take a few deep breaths and remember your intention.

PRACTICE GRATITUDE: Be thankful for your food and for all the people and forces that brought it to your table: the sun that shone down on it, the farmer who grew it and the waiter who delivered it. Taking a moment to give thanks will calm you and remind you of your connection to the whole. It will also enable you to feel grateful for real, healthy food and simple pleasures.

ENJOY: Whatever you choose to eat—even if you know it is not perfectly healthy—allow yourself to enjoy it. Guilt is a stressor that makes you, and your digestive system, unhappy.

EXPERIMENT: It's that bio-individuality thing again. Experiment with different dietary theories and foods so that over time you can discover what works best for you and your body. At the very least, eat a few meals each week with no animal products by ordering proteins such as beans. Whatever you do, eat your veggies!

SOCIAL SITUATIONS
Even with the best intentions you will occasionally end up at a restaurant that does not serve healthy food and/or with a group of diners who do not share your dietary goals. What to do?

ORDER SIDES: Most restaurants have a selection of side dishes that you can create a meal out of, such as vegetables and a whole grain.

SPECIAL ORDER: An accommodating, creative chef will be happy to make something especially for you. Try requests like: "I know it's not on the menu, but could you put together a plate of vegetables and beans for me?" or "I'd like an extra-large version of your side salad as my entrée."

SKIP THE FREEBIES: Just because the bread is complimentary does not mean that you have to eat it. Likewise, try to ignore those fortune cookies or mints that arrive with the bill.

ASK FOR SAUCE ON THE SIDE: If the salad dressings and sauces are not up to par, ask for the waitstaff to bring them on the side so that you can monitor how much you use.

ASK FOR SUBSTITUTIONS: Some restaurants charge for doing this, and some don't. In any case, it is worth asking for things like green veggies or even boiled potatoes instead of french fries.

I hope to have left you with enough inspiration, motivation and education to put my five precepts into action. It's time to start enjoying your food more than ever while getting healthier at the same time. You *can* have your naturally sweetened dessert and eat it too. So let's get to the best part (I have a feeling you may have taken a peek already) and check out the restaurants.

THE RESTAURANTS

Icon Key

$

Meals for 1 (including beverage, tax, and tip) under $10

$ $

$11–$30

$ $ $

$31–$60

$ $

above $60

Vegetarian menu

Primarily meat-based menu

Vegan menu

Macrobiotic menu

Raw menu

Gluten-free options

Naturally sweetened desserts

Nearby subways

ABIGAIL

New American
807 Classon Ave. (@ St. Johns Pl.)

⑤ ② ③ ④ ⑤

718 399-3200
abigailbrooklyn.com
Sun–Thu: 10am–11pm
Fri–Sat: 10am–12am

Abigail in Prospect Heights takes the concept of nourishing, tasty food at affordable prices one step further; here, unexpected spices and exotic flavors are infused into fresh local dishes. This corner restaurant with its spacious tables, glowing red light fixtures and book-lined shelves is the type of place to happily settle in for a few hours of conversation with good friends and good food.

On one sultry evening, a relaxed meal began with the Abigail summer salad, a fresh toss of ripe peaches, bright beets, greens and thin slivers of red onion. Chef Abby Hitchcock's talent for unusual flavor marriages shone in the curry dusted grilled calamari appetizer. However, this dish was compelling in concept but faltered in execution—while the aroma was enticing, a chewy texture left me wishing I had selected another of the plentiful tempting options. This one misstep didn't take away from the cozy and memorable atmosphere, further enhanced by a smiling staff and attentive owners. The moment a candle went out, owner Jason was at our table to revive the ambiance with a lighter. Next came wholesome entrées, including market fish over ratatouille finished with bright sauce verte. We chose the arctic char over the bass, and we were glad we did; the char was moist and expertly seared, perched on top of the slow-roasted ratatouille. Cumin-crusted pork tenderloin was flawless, resting on a bed of fresh summer corn pudding, topped with a tangle of Tuscan kale. The cumin seasoning of this hearty dish brought a layer of the exotic to a comforting, country-style dish.

Choose Abigail if you want to casually devour some serious food: sit back, relax and dine to the sounds of live acoustic guitar at this Prospect Heights hangout.

JESSICA COLLEY

If you like Italian food, you may come to believe that Al Di La is the best restaurant in Brooklyn.

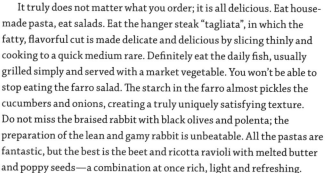

AL DI LA TRATTORIA
Italian
248 5th Ave. (@ Carroll St.) Ⓡ
718 783-4565
aldilatrattoria.com
Mon, Wed–Thu: 12pm–3pm, 6pm–10:30pm
Fri: 12pm–3pm, 6pm–11pm
Sat: 11am–3:30pm, 5:30pm–10:30pm
Sun: 11am–3:30pm, 5pm–10pm

It is lovingly decorated, with burnt orange and yellow wall and curtain tones to offset antiqued wooden furniture and flower-embossed plate ware. It is peaceful inside Al Di La even when it is packed, which is p conceived and carefully prepared; at the same time, it is pure and rustic and bursting with flavor, and it feels effortless, which enhances the authenticity of the dining experience.

It truly does not matter what you order; it is all delicious. Eat house-made pasta, eat salads. Eat the hanger steak "tagliata", in which the fatty, flavorful cut is made delicate and delicious by slicing thinly and cooking to a quick medium rare. Definitely eat the daily fish, usually grilled simply and served with a market vegetable. You won't be able to stop eating the farro salad. The starch in the farro almost pickles the cucumbers and onions, creating a truly uniquely satisfying texture. Do not miss the braised rabbit with black olives and polenta; the preparation of the lean and gamy rabbit is unbeatable. All the pastas are fantastic, but the best is the beet and ricotta ravioli with melted butter and poppy seeds—a combination at once rich, light and refreshing.

Al Di La does not take reservations. They take your name and phone number, tell you your wait time and send you to their wine bar (and extension of the restaurant) around the corner. Try to avoid being seated there, (it lacks the provincial charm of the main restaurant) but happily accept a compensatory glass of prosecco when the wait for your table drags on longer than promised. Just wait and sip—it will be worth it.

TALIA BERMAN

ALCHEMY

American

56 5th Ave. (Bergen St. & St. Marks Pl.)

Ⓑ Ⓓ Ⓝ Ⓠ Ⓡ ② ③ ④ ⑤

718 636-4385

alchemybrooklyn.com

Mon–Thu: 9am–11pm

Fri: 9am–12am

Sat: 10am–12am

Sun: 10am–11pm

Alchemy is easy to like. Modeled after townhouse gastropubs of Hampstead, London, it is carefully decorated and caringly looked after. Equally low-key, unpretentious and classy, the fare is upscale pub meets French bistro with a sprinkling of American classics. The bartender calls out a greeting when you walk in the door, so grab a stool at the 100-year-old refurbished bar, nestle into one of the huge banquettes, or introduce yourself to your neighbors at one of Alchemy's communal tables. Then you can figure out what you want to eat. Don't over think it—the simple dishes are the best.

Among these simple dishes is a great burger: grass-fed Angus beef with onion brioche and shallot confit. The salads, beets with goat cheese and almonds, a standard Caesar and a steak salad with blue cheese and red onions (lunch only), are unadventurous yet satisfying. The entrées are delicious, particularly the hanger steak, grilled simply with black pepper and herbed butter and served alongside crunchy sautéed kale. For vegetarian-leaning diners, the shells and cheese are tender and rich. Peas, bacon and breadcrumbs make this Midwestern comfort food new again.

Alchemy is open for breakfast, which makes it one of the only alternatives to diners and bagel stores in the area. For especially hungry breakfasters, the Swiss breakfast includes smoked salmon, an over-easy egg, roasted potatoes, toast, sour cream, capers and onions. Try the tofu scramble with fillings of your choice; flavorful and filling, this is one of the better tofu preparations around.

Open for breakfast, lunch and dinner, it is no surprise to anyone that Alchemy has garnered a sizable neighborhood following. Thankfully it even maintains its mellow vibe on Sunday mornings when the line is out the door and the plates are flying out of the kitchen.

TALIA BERMAN

Try and keep your attention on your company rather than the wholesome food at Applewood in Park Slope. Flavors here encourage curiosity, prompt questions and often steal your focus from your date. As I smeared white bean puree on whole-wheat bread, I couldn't help but wonder what gave the

APPLEWOOD
New American

501 11th St. (7th & 8th Ave.) (F) (G)
718 788-1810
applewoodny.com
Tue–Fri: 5pm–11pm
Sat: 10am–2pm, 5pm–11pm
Sun: 10am–3pm

puree such a pleasant heat. Our knowledgeable server sauntered over to refill the water glasses and informed us that pickled chilies infused complexity into the humble spread. Much like the white bean puree, I liked Applewood immediately.

After a day in the chaotic city, who wouldn't be drawn to the country-style chairs, sprigs of lavender on the table and warm lighting? There's also a fireplace crackling during winter, as if the rest of the country charm wasn't enough to seduce diners. But more than the décor, the thoughtful food left a firm impression upon me.

My meal began with the mixed green salad: a generous plate of greens punctuated by bursts of fresh cherries, crumbly house-made ricotta and thyme-infused honey. Ambitious combinations continued with the first bite of Rhode Island scallops, accented with the zing of charred cherry peppers, sour milk dumplings and vanilla-scented fumé. Next came expertly pan roasted Atlantic striped bass, served crispy skin-side up over toasted wheat berries, grilled onions and sweet roasted carrot puree. We snagged the last order of grilled juicy New Hampshire pork—described as luscious by my dining companion—with a rustic cannellini bean ragout, summer spinach and sorrel chimichurri as a finishing polish. The Sheas, the chef plus front-of-house power couple, are devoted to supporting local farmers and serving sustainable seafood and hormone-free meats and poultry. With a constantly changing menu, it won't be any easier concentrating on your date next time you visit Applewood: there will be more questions that need delicious answers.

JESSICA COLLEY

AURORA
Italian
70 Grand St. (@ Wythe Ave.)

Ⓛ Ⓙ Ⓜ Ⓩ Ⓖ

718 388-5100
auroraristorante.com
Mon–Thu: 12pm–3:30pm, 6pm–11pm
Fri: 12pm–3:30pm, 6pm–12am
Sat: 11am–4pm, 6pm–12am
Sun: 11am–4pm, 5pm–10pm
(Cash Only)

When you dine at a trattoria on a romantic southern Italian coast (whether in dream or actuality), there are romances you can expect: smells of ocean water in the air, the bounty it contains transformed on your plate, the background din of produce vendors shouting "Pomodori qui!" and "Ha funghi!" over each other, and the click-click-click of fancy heels expertly navigating the cobblestoned streets.

At Aurora, you can almost glimpse the Williamsburg waterfront from the street. There are no cobblestones (or very many stiletto-clad pedestrians); alas, there are no perfect tomatoes for sale "qui" on this quiet street in Brooklyn. And yet somehow, the food translates.

Different seasons bring different incarnations of a straightforward southern Italian menu: Antipasti (salads, carpaccio, flatbread), Primi (pastas with various seasonal vegetables) and Secondi (fish of the day, roasted half-chicken, steak, lamb chop).

Portions are generous—an heirloom tomato salad with burrata, basil and breadcrumbs was almost too big to finish, but we did, because not much is better than an heirloom tomato with olive oil and sea salt in the middle of August. The fish of the day, a whole Mediterranean sea bass, was flaky, fresh and an enormous portion for one person; plus, it was abundantly outfitted with steamed broccoli rabe and olive oil-crushed potatoes. There is spicy puttanesca, heavy on the chopped oregano and parsley, buoyed in this version with Setaro durum wheat bucatini and bits of swordfish. The sauce is tasty, but the puttanesca lacks a dousing of olive oil or pasta water to bring the flavors together.

Dining at Aurora is nice. The outdoor garden is quaint, and the staff is friendly and unassuming. The food is good to great, comfortable, authentic-feeling Italian—you almost won't miss that Almalfi sunset.

TALIA BERMAN

Local art and a globe pay tribute to Olivier Jimenez and Paulina Abd-el-Kader's Clinton Hill home, French roots and the trip around the world (Autour du Monde) that inspired their eclectic cuisine.

Autour du Monde's dark wood furniture and casual, lounge-like atmosphere don't leave a huge impression; they let the food (and Jimenez) do the talking—global with a heavy French accent. The kitchen is stocked with fresh, sustainable and local ingredients, a fact which Jimenez was eager to share.

Jimenez makes first-time guests feel at once like esteemed VIPs and neighborhood regulars. He's charmingly—and understandably—proud of his restaurant's food. Global bistro eats range from the classic comforts to upscale innovations or, as in a frisée salad with turkey bacon, poached egg and avocado yogurt dressing, both. Cabbage and carrot strips in steamed rice wraps were enjoyably restrained with the exception of a too-salty sauce at the plate's center. We turned the veggie cakes (normally an entrée) into an oversized starter. A lovely mélange of carrots, shallots, edamame, herbs and quinoa with a hint of binding potato, the gently crisped cakes came with a bland but well-cooked side of baby bok choy.

With a surprisingly steak-like façade, the blackened pan-roasted duck was light pink within. Fig vinaigrette imparted sweet acidity to the meat, while a frisée salad and roasted potatoes balanced the dish. A mild cod came to life with house-made arugula pesto, a fantastically bright puree of almond, orange and arugula. A citrusy basmati rice with soft, julienned zucchini and carrots made for a pleasant side.

For such quality, the menu is forgivingly priced, especially if you go for the nightly three-course prix fixe. Full of flavor that's never too weighty, Autour du Monde weaves the world into one Brooklyn wonder.

JACLYN EINIS

AUTOUR DU MONDE
French
860 Fulton St. (@ Clinton Ave.)
Ⓐ Ⓒ Ⓖ
718 398-3500
restaurantautourdumonde.com
Tue–Fri: 4pm–10:30pm
Sat–Sun: 10:30am–11pm

BARE BURGER
New American, Fast Food
170 7th Ave. (@ 1st St.)
Ⓑ Ⓠ ② ③ ④ Ⓕ Ⓖ
718 768-2273
bareburger.com
Sun–Thu: 11am–11pm
Fri–Sat: 11am–12am

Brooklynites initially had to leave their beloved borough to get their Bare Burgers. Now, Park Slope residents can get their delicious grass-fed burgers just steps from Grand Army Plaza.

The menu abounds with options, so your carb-free friend, vegetarian buddy, sustainable carnivore and adventurous foodie will all be satisfied. There are nine styles of burgers to pick from as well as a small list of rotating specials. Choose the bun—brioche, 7-grain, wrap, or a lettuce wrap; the burger—beef, turkey, chicken, veggie, portabella mushroom, bison, elk, or even ostrich; and a slew of cheeses, toppings, sides and condiments (including organic ketchup).

Their namesake is the Original Bare Burger, made from Piedmontese beef with a thin mantle of cheese, shredded iceberg lettuce, tomato, red onion and a tasty special sauce. Though classic, there are more interesting options. A spicy bacon elk burger drips with flavor while the veggie burger is an especially moist patty of grains and legumes, made buttery with avocado.

If dining with fork and knife is your style (not to mention a good way to get in your greens), there are a handful of salads on the menu. The baby arugula, Pepper Jack cheese, avocado and walnut salad we tried was a little underdressed but could make a meal with all of the fixings.

Little touches like agave nectar for sweetening coffee and tea, various dipping sauces and a kid's menu show that Bare Burger is eager to please. With all of the options it is easy to overindulge; remember, even organic, it's still a milkshake. Nevertheless, if you can't resist the burger, fries and shake trinity, then it may as well be at an organic, eco-conscious restaurant that has low-energy toilets and walls lined with sustainable cork. This is guilt-free fast food at its best.

SCARLETT LINDEMAN

Despite its central location just a few blocks from the populous Bedford Ave. L station, this suitably named bar and restaurant is quite tranquil once inside. Don't let the dim lighting, no-frills wooden decor and couples sipping beer and cocktails fool you—The Bedford may appear to be a quiet spot for post-work drinking, but it happens

THE BEDFORD
New American
110 Bedford Ave. (@ N. 11th St.) Ⓛ
718 302-1002
thebedfordonbedford.com
Mon–Thu: 8am–4pm, 6pm–11pm
Fri: 8am–4pm, 6pm–12am
Sat: 11:30am–4pm, 6pm–12am
Sun: 11:30am–4pm, 6pm–11pm

to offer an excellent and frequently changing menu that should not be overlooked. The three starters we sampled are a great way to either begin a meal or accompany a happy hour (or late-night) drink. The Colorado lamb ribs were crisp on the outside and tender on the inside, the lamb lending its distinct gaminess to the typically porcine snack. Lightly fried artichokes were golden in color and complemented by a pucker-inducing Meyer lemon and Greek yogurt dip. Also share-worthy are the local bluefish tacos, topped with cool Mexican crema, lettuce and crunchy pickled onions in addition to the generous portion of fish. Should you opt to stay for dinner (a wise choice), the pasture-raised burger and beer-braised Niman Ranch pork are fine selections. My only beef with the burger (pun not intended) was that its interior was a bit rarer than the requested medium rare, but the patty's very flavorful meat managed to redeem the dish. The pork was fork-tender and delicious, though the ho-hum spaetzle served beneath it proved much less memorable. To offset these protein and carb-heavy entrées, green sides (we went for the garlic-infused wild spinach) are available as well. Not only can patrons choose between sharing small plates among friends or enjoying a sit-down dinner, but luckily the oft-rotating menu promises an unexpected (and tasty) variety of food to distinguish each visit.   ALLIX GENESLAW

BEER TABLE
New American
427B 7th Ave. (14th & 15th St.)
(F) (G) (R)
718 965-1196
beertable.com
Daily: 5pm–1am

It is called "Beer Table," and if you don't look carefully, you might miss the kitchen tucked away behind the elaborate line of seven drafts, 25 bottles and a cask. The location is not tiny, with room for about 25 at three long, high counters, and with such profound attention to beers of all varieties, it is quite possible to completely miss any food.

But that omission would be a shame, because the food at Beer Table is wonderful. The snacks are fun and quirky. Try the pickled sea beans and dehydrated tomatoes; they are crispy and chewy all at once.

Once you've snacked sufficiently, move on to the generous appetizers and entrées. They are satisfying and delicious, but don't over think them—their success is in their simplicity.

First try the ricotta on toast with honey, black pepper and seasonal fruit to cut through the rich cheese. Roasted beets with arugula and pickled baby fennel are also rich, but this time, richly sweet. The beets narrowly avoid a cloying pucker when paired with bitter arugula and a tart fennel crunch. Entrées are hearty enough to stand up to the beer, and they all contain meat even if it's not the main event (the butter beans are flavored with bacon and scallions, served on slices of doughy bread). The beef and pork chili with pickled jalapenos and red onions is a perfect winter's day companion, missing only a cold stout pint with which to wash it down.

Beer Table is known for its brunch which, like dinner, is barebones but sufficient. The light-n-fluffy waffles are the stars here with two options for toppings: ricotta and blueberries or butter and sea salt. The latter is the better preparation—let the simplicity win again, and you will not be disappointed.

TALIA BERMAN

A nod to the Parisian neighborhood of the same name, Belleville ("beautiful town") brings the casual beauty of a French brasserie to Park Slope. Patio doors give Fifth Avenue passersby a peek into the corner bistro. From the French-imported deco-cut bar to the worn white tiled floor and menu-ridden mirrors,

BELLEVILLE
French
330-332 5th St. (@ 5th Ave.)
Ⓓ Ⓝ Ⓡ Ⓕ Ⓖ
718 832-9777
bellevillebistro.com
Mon–Fri: 5pm–11pm
Sat–Sun: 10:30am–4pm, 5pm–11pm

Belleville does a flawless rendition of retro bistro.

Our first courses lived up to the space's aesthetic finesse. Served with sushi-platter elegance, a cumulus burrata arrived alongside bread slices and a small bowl of yellow and red cherry tomatoes on a wooden board. The Atlantic salmon tartare's Asian touch came in its delicious flavor: large pieces of fresh fish were marinated alongside avocado with soy, ginger and a touch of sesame oil.

Classic French preparations of sustainable meats and fish dominate less refined entrées. Beef short ribs were slow braised to spoonworthy tenderness and served with spring onions, haricot verts and creamy soft polenta. My tongue searched for the fresh horseradish in the jus, but the spice drowned in the heady meat. We were disappointed by the Hudson Valley duck leg confit, which, in spite of the dish's inherent fattiness, was stringy-dry. Its saving graces were its accoutrements: a handful of spring gnocchi, sweet glazed pearl onions, market vegetables, pancetta bits and frisée with aged balsamic. The one vegetarian entrée, also available as a starter, rose above the meats. Wild shimeji mushrooms, baby arugula, walnuts and Parmesan boosted otherwise mild acorn squash gnocchi. The browned-but-puffy light-within handmade dumplings brought additional textural excitement to the dish.

Where Belleville does well, it truly excels. It'd be more than worth a return trip to explore the rest of Park Slope's Paris.   JACLYN EINIS

BENCHMARK
New American

339A 2nd St. (@ 5th Ave.)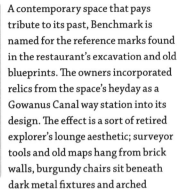
718 965-7040
benchmarkrestaurant.com
Mon: 11:30am–3pm, 5pm–10pm
Tue–Thu: 11:30am–3pm, 5pm–11pm
Fri: 11:30am–3pm, 5pm–12am
Sat: 10am–3pm, 5pm–12am
Sun: 10am–3pm, 5pm–10pm

A contemporary space that pays tribute to its past, Benchmark is named for the reference marks found in the restaurant's excavation and old blueprints. The owners incorporated relics from the space's heyday as a Gowanus Canal way station into its design. The effect is a sort of retired explorer's lounge aesthetic; surveyor tools and old maps hang from brick walls, burgundy chairs sit beneath dark metal fixtures and arched windows overlook a spacious garden.

And how do Brooklyn's retired navigators sate their appetite these days? Through contemporary steakhouse cuisine with an eco-bent. Crisp yuca, black pepper, goat cheese and roasted strawberries dotted a salad of organic seasonal lettuces. I longed to taste more of the delicious berries and modestly sprinkled truffle vinaigrette, but the pepper overpowered both. The spicy lobster salad was innovative but overambitious. Too-small pieces of fresh lobster were wasted, lost among the overwhelming tropicality of hearts of palm, a wacky banana guacamole and spicy-sweet coconut dressing.

Though vegetarian entrées are available, "creature" comforts are at the menu's core. A grass-fed filet mignon was lean, tender and straightforward with a few unctuous bites of caramelized marrow and mashed potatoes (instead of the menu's promised purple potato gratin) on the side. However, we wanted more than a streak of the parsley pesto which added a necessary hit of flavor to the plate. A substantial seared ahi tuna didn't blow me away, but I appreciated its turn away from the usual Asian accompaniments. Crusted with black-trumpet mushrooms, it arrived with fresh salsify and an earthy mix of pickled chanterelles and charred mushroom jus.

Next time you're craving some pasture-raised (or wild-caught) protein in Park Slope, set your sights on the benchmarks off Fifth Avenue and 2nd.

JACLYN EINIS

Imagine a slice joint reinvented by the Beastie Boys. That's Best Pizza, a collaboration between the guys at cult favorite Bushwick spot Roberta's and the Momofuku-trained chef-owner of Williamsburg's Brooklyn Star. Doodles on paper plates wallpaper the bright, airy space (even the

BEST PIZZA
Italian, Fast Food
33 Havemeyer St. (N. 7th & N. 8th St.)
Ⓛ

718 599-2210
best.piz.za.com
Sun–Fri: 12pm–12am
Sat: 12pm–1am

ceiling!). Hip-hop music plays at deafening volume. The menu board is short on options, long on 'tude. And why not? When you're preparing the basics this carefully, you've earned a little attitude.

Pizza man Frank Pinello hails from za-savvy Bensonhurst, and he's also a graduate of the Culinary Institute of America. A long, slow rise gives his dough heft and tang. Anchovies give the sauce on his square pie a salty, funky punch. Pies come in three varieties: regular cheese, a thin, crisp crust topped with crushed tomatoes and mild, house-made mozzarella; lightly-cheesed white, elevated by sweetly caramelized onions and the surprise of a sesame seeded crust; and grandma, a square pie that's thinner than Sicilian but with a chewy, buttery crunch featuring that anchovy-laced, garlicky sauce and fresh, milky mozz. All are fired in a century-old, wood-burning brick oven, creating the char and crackle prized by pizza aficionados. The "farmers' market" inspires the veggie slice—fiddlehead ferns for springtime and thinly shaved summer squash in August.

Best also offers two sandwiches: a meatball sub with delicate-yet-hearty balls made from Pat LaFrieda beef and browned (in that same oven) then topped with a dollop of grandma sauce and sharp Pecorino cheese. Be warned, an inconsistent hand with the salt shaker means that occasionally, this can be a salt bomb—and a chicken parm, made with tender, brined, organic thigh meat, breaded and fried to order.

Clearly, this isn't traditional health food. But if you're looking for an inexpensive, fast and conscious indulgence, Best Pizza lives up to its name.   DEBBIE KOENIG

BLISS CAFÉ
New American
191 Bedford Ave. (N. 6th & N. 7th St.)

718 599-2547
No website
Mon–Fri: 9am–11pm
Sat–Sun: 10am–11pm
(Cash Only)

Part café, part restaurant: Bliss Café is home to both stragglers who type away on their Macbooks as well as diners who crave a "home-cooked" vegan or vegetarian meal. The quirky, eclectic decor gives the tiny interior its coffee shop feel—the ceiling is lined with pressed tin, while the walls are covered with a blend of funky paintings, ads for local businesses and multicolored patterns. Whether you join the graphic designers and grad students or the hungry commuters who stumble off the nearby L train, Bliss conveniently awaits with an organic coffee and maple-sweetened snack—or, if you're looking for something more substantial, a heaping plate of greens, proteins and whole grains.

The menu is extensive and at first seems too ambitious, but after sampling an array of dishes, it is obvious that Bliss has mastered versatility. The Bliss Salad alone could cure scurvy—whole strawberries, avocado and tomato wedges, cucumber slices and julienned granny smith apples and carrots top a massive bed of organic mixed greens. The grilled portobello and zucchini sandwich is sufficiently stuffed and perfect for a quick lunch, its ingredients retaining plenty of bite and flavor. While the panini references Italian seasoning with its pesto spread, the pasta special is a garlic-infused nod to Asia. Tender carrots, broccoli, cauliflower and onions encircle a tangled mass of soba noodles. Owing allegiance to no region in particular, the harvest bowl welcomes interaction among its balanced ingredients. Cornbread and brown rice sop up a robust stew left behind by organic lentils, and kale and cooked vegetables can be further enhanced by vegan dressing (go for the lemon tahini miso). Main courses can be topped with your choice of protein— grilled tempeh, tofu, or seitan.

Carnivores beware: a trip to Bliss may produce some vegan and vegetarian converts.   ALLIX GENESLAW

Court Street touts many cozy and intimate restaurants, and Brucie's is a happy addition to the bunch. As we stepped into the restaurant, homey rustic charm welcomed us with lemony-colored walls, a beautiful white and blue tiled wall, built-in bookshelves holding old cookbooks and simple wood tables topped with candles and salt and pepper shakers. How could it get more charming? The restaurant's name is inspired by the owner's pooches: Burrito + Lucy = Brucie's.

BRUCIE
Italian
234 Court St. (Baltic & Kane St.)
347 987-4961
brucienyc.com
Tue–Thu: 12pm–3:30pm, 5pm–10pm
Fri–Sat: 12pm–3:30pm, 5pm–11pm

On the simple yet varied menu, house-made pastas like tagliatelle and pappardelle shone next to likewise house-made burrata, mozzarella and ricotta. Pork comes from Lancaster Farms in Pennsylvania and produce from a nearby farm in Prospect Heights. While the menu changes daily, our waiter informed us that there are a few veteran dishes including the sandwiches, spaghetti, market caesar salad, a tagliatelle dish, a type of scallop dish and a pork belly dish.

Most of the appetizers and sides we tried sadly proved to be too oily; the mozzarella and tomato pastries came wrapped in warm, flaky phyllo dough and were a bit too decadent. The house-made papardelle however, with tomatoes, zucchini ribbons and sweet corn was sublime. The noodles were perfectly al dente, the produce fresh and when combined with the tomato sauce, revealed to us the pastas as the shining stars of Brucie's menu. We also enjoyed the roast pork with collard greens and nectarine agrodolce atop creamy polenta. Spices like clove and star anise seasoned the meat, but while the dish was certainly flavorful, it was a bit heavy on the salt for our tastes.

Although Brucie's stumbles across the traps of daily menu changes, a few things are certain—its pastas are stellar, the ambiance casual yet intimate and the service is genuinely kind.   AMY SUNG

BUBBY'S
American
1 Main St.
718 222-0666
bubbys.com
Mon–Fri: 9am–11pm
Sat–Sun: 9am–4pm

Maybe it's my Semitic upbringing, but the Yiddish term "bubby" conjures terrifying images of a chesty matron cloaked in an ill-fitting housedress, orthopedic slippers and her own (hormone-filled) chicken soup recipe bravado. Bubby's menu, however, encouraged me to reevaluate my stringent definition of the word—barbecue, which is slow-smoked on the premises using local hogs and wood, is the porky specialty. A section of the menu lists its New York state sources and describes its pesticide-free and environmentally friendly allegiance.

The basin-sized barbecue sampler includes pulled pork, ribs and a hot link and comes with two sides (sautéed spinach and baked beans, in our case). This meal is not for those who shy away from sodium; I fancy myself an ardent sodium fan and still clutched my naturally sweetened soda after each salty bite. Of the three piggy barbecue options, the pulled pork was my favorite—hot pepper flakes punctuated the sizable pile, giving it a nice degree of heat. The grass-fed burger, also mammoth in size, was cooked to a ruddy medium rare; its juices forming a beefy puddle for the crisp fries. The greens were equally plentiful and fresh. Spinach is delicious as a side or salad—the former is sautéed with ample amounts of garlic; the latter cool, crisp and topped with thick-cut bacon. The buttermilk dressing (best ordered on the side) is sharp and milky, but if applied too liberally its gloppy consistency might overwhelm the vibrant greens. It seems I now have two bubbies to feed me till I'm incapacitated, though thankfully the latter employs ingredients that won't simultaneously fill my body with noxious chemicals.

ALLIX GENESLAW

Before visiting Burger Guru in Williamsburg, I didn't know there was a spiritual path to the perfect burger. Yet it quickly became clear that this Greek-inspired restaurant is destined to be a mentor for healthy, high-quality burgers. Owner Nick Voulkoudis

THE BURGER GURU
American
98 Berry St. (@ N. 8th St.)
718 599-4878
theburgerguru.com
Mon–Fri: 11:30am–11pm
Sat–Sun: 11am–Close

has gained attention for serving a range of meats on a brioche bun. Natural meat purveyor Pat LaFrieda provides the blends that allow this guru to shed light on the humble hamburger.

The food philosophy dates back over 100 years to Great-Grandfather Leonidas, famous for his naturally-raised cattle and tasty burgers in the foothills of the Greek Pindus Mountains. This devotion to quality is equally apparent today. My meal began with the baby greens salad, tossed with crunchy walnuts, smooth goat cheese, bright beets and finished with a white balsamic vinaigrette. Greek roots shone through with a kalamata olive dip for house-made organic corn chips, perfectly thick with a lovely crunch.

The burgers are served on blue and white checked paper in quaint stainless steel pans. They claim to serve the ultimate burger, and happily, the Burger Guru delivered. The harmonious "sunshine burger" balances arugula, avocado and tomato atop a bison patty and was distinctly leaner than its beef counterpart. The turkey burger was equally flavorful with sweet caramelized onions and a tangy BBQ sauce.

Sampling exotic proteins is half the fun. Antelope, lamb and ostrich can all be substituted (seasonally) for an organic beef burger, and on the day I arrived, an alligator option was available. The meat was peppery and intermingled with tomato, pickles and shredded lettuce for a delicious adventure. Vegetarians can visit the guru as well for a garden or Portobello burger.

The Burger Guru awaits you in Williamsburg, ready to shed some light on your regular burger routine and expand your horizons. Grandpa Leonidas would have been proud.   JESSICA COLLEY

BUTTERMILK CHANNEL
New American
524 Court St. (@ Huntington St.) Ⓕ Ⓖ
718 852-8490
buttermilkchannelnyc.com
Mon–Thu: 5pm–11pm
Fri: 5pm–12am
Sat: 10am–12am
Sun: 10am–11pm

Buttermilk Channel is a local restaurant. The name refers to the body of water separating Brooklyn from Governors' Island. All the wine they serve is from the United States, and there is a preponderance of vintners from Long Island and the Finger Lakes. Local celebrities like Sofia Coppola like to drop in for brunch to sit outside in the café and watch the strollers roll by.

They keep coming back for the food, which is careful, consistently delicious and impressively versatile. Side-by-side on the menu are buttermilk-fried chicken and waffles and a sophisticated warm lamb and romaine salad with capers and a soft-boiled egg. From the charcuterie there is mustard-glazed grilled bacon, and entrées like the duck meatloaf and the Delmonico rib eye are tributes to the animals they come from. At the same time, Buttermilk Channel has a separate vegetarian menu that is a conglomeration of vegetarian dishes from the main menu, bulked up with a few additional options. The vegetarian dishes are the stars of the restaurant, with home runs like the cranberry bean and fennel stew, steaming with somehow-still-crispy fingerling potatoes and braised greens. The meatless versions of Buttermilk mainstays—the cheddar waffles served with roasted mushrooms and sweet peas and warm mozzarella and romaine salad with roasted cauliflower and a soft-boiled egg are every bit as tasty as the animal incarnations.

While dining at Buttermilk Channel, one feels taken care of—from the separate vegetarian menu to the veritable stack of strollers waiting for crying children (ubiquitous in the neighborhood) to the foam glued to the bottom of your chair to minimize sound (it really works!), everything at Buttermilk Channel is designed with you in mind. The staff is friendly and nonchalant, the décor is elegant and informal and the scene is jovial—and none of it is incidental.   TALIA BERMAN

In Italy, cooking with the seasons has been a way of life for generations. This tradition of seasonality receives a touch of polish at Broken English, a Cobble Hill Italian restaurant full of mismatched vintage chairs, exposed brick walls and a long, attractive bar. Beyond nailing the warmth of Italian hospitality (the gracious atmosphere here

BROKEN ENGLISH
Italian
68 Bergen St. (Smith & Court St.)

718 488-3906
brokenenglishbrooklyn.com
Mon–Fri: 11:30am–3pm,
5:30pm–10:30pm
Sat: 12pm–10:30pm
Sun: 1pm–10:30pm

encourages lingering meals that are reminiscent of Italian family meals), this restaurant also nails the commitment to fresh ingredients and the beauty of simple combinations that are staples of the best Italian cuisine.

Our impeccable meal began with a lovely salad, mixing peppery arugula with the burst of red grapes, the tang of blue cheese and the fragrant crunch of toasted pecans. Small meatballs—made of all natural beef, veal, pork and ricotta—were packed with flavorful herbs and topped with a light tomato sauce. Pastas are also available as appetizers and are perfectly portioned to share, including an immaculate roasted butternut squash agnolotti, tossed with chunky spears of crunchy asparagus. If you would rather dine on pasta as your entrée, choose the whole wheat pappardelle with meaty wild mushrooms and bright fava beans folded into the al dente pasta; I didn't want to share a bite of this divine dish.

The proteins also shine at Broken English, including grilled Cornish hen, marinated in rosemary, mustard, sage, red pepper flakes and parsley. This dish showed devotion to a slow kind of cooking, one where complex flavors are the marvelous result of time. This welcoming, breezy, restaurant might be called Broken English, but here you can work on your broken Italian while ordering everything from insalata di rughetta to papperdelle ai funghi. JESSICA COLLEY

CAFÉ GHIA
French
24 Irving Ave. (@ Troutman St.) Ⓛ
718 821-8806
cafeghia.com
Daily: 10am–12am
(Cash Only)

In an overwhelming city, Café Ghia makes things easy. Walk one block from the L train's Jefferson stop and look for the The Family Restaurant sign, an homage to the space's former owner.

This sweet corner spot's cozy, laid-back vibe will make you want to stick around. Settle in at one of a handful of tables or on a stool alongside the diner-style bar. Owners Scott McGibney and Anna D'Agrosa like to keep things local; they also live in Bushwick and source from as close to home as possible. The small but well-varied seasonal menu includes mainstays like the tempeh reuben and a grass-fed burger.

We began with the kale salad, whose lemon–kimchi vinaigrette added a bite of acid to the greens with just-funky-enough kimchi. Grilled slices of white and wheat bread and a paltry serving of green beans and carrots accompanied our tasty choice of dips: hummus and almond-topped cauliflower puree (all condiments are house-made).

Luckily, I got my hands on a few more green beans, served in miso sauce with our seared scallops. Crispy on top, the scallops were enjoyably buttery in texture but too much so in flavor. Everything on the plate—from the shellfish to the carrot citrus puree and lemon emulsion surrounding them—seemed to be inundated with the stuff.

Steering clear of the bacon-fat-infused burger, we opted for the roasted chicken sandwich and never looked back. Its soft, pesto-brushed challah roll hugged the pasture-raised chicken, juicy heirloom tomatoes and Manchego cheese. Fresh organic greens provided a lighter side for the delectable sandwich than the alternative roasted herbed potatoes.

I'm excited to see Café Ghia evolve with the seasons, and I'll be back soon to try their intriguing brunch. Vegan scramble with ginger-lime tofu "cream" and crispy millet cakes? Count me in. JACLYN EINIS

A tiny, unassuming kitchen attached to a downtown Brooklyn grocery isn't the typical location for a two Michelin-starred restaurant. Yet, Chef's Table at Brooklyn Fare continues to break the culinary mold. Since opening in late 2010, snagging one of the eighteen seats at this exclusive supper club has become one of the city's most coveted reservations. If you

CHEF'S TABLE AT BROOKLYN FARE
New American
200 Schermerhorn St.
(Hoyt & Bond St.)
Ⓐ Ⓒ Ⓖ ② ③ ④ ⑤
718 243-0050
brooklynfare.com
Tue–Sat: 7pm–Close

happen to be lucky (or mighty persistent) enough to attend a nightly dinner seating, you'll enter an intimate room filled by a stainless steel U-shaped communal table facing hanging copper pots and a state-of-the-art open kitchen.

Focusing on seasonal ingredients, chef Cesar Ramirez and staff gracefully prepare a well-paced procession of 18-20 small plates, varying daily based on produce availability. Flavorful amuses awakened my taste buds, such as succulent king crab meat wrapped in delicate shredded phyllo atop chilled cucumber dill yogurt and a cube of flaky Japanese fluke that arrived under a sliver of tart pickled daikon. After about a dozen singular bites (the majority fish-based), seven larger courses followed, including a lightly seasoned rouget over Japanese risotto in foamy saffron bouillabaisse and the most beautifully cooked duck I've ever had—tender with thinly fat-laden crispy skin, balanced by earthy chanterelles and silky miso purée. Succeeding an onslaught of savory, I welcomed a creamy fromage blanc sorbet melting into a pool of sweet cherries laced with yuzu rind.

No detail went overlooked, down to the attentive service and exquisite handmade china collection. With a BYO policy, don't forget your favorite bottle (no corkage fee) and be prepared to eat whatever's put in front of you—the chef's not known for customizing the menu. Worth the price and hassle to get in, this truly is a dining experience of a lifetime. MEGAN MURPHY

CHESTNUT
New American
271 Smith St. (Degraw & Sackett St.)

718 243-0049
chestnutonsmith.com
Tue–Sat: 5:30pm–11pm
Sun: 11:30am–3pm, 5:30pm–10pm

In non-vegetarian restaurants, meatless entrées tend to be enormous, as if the chef wants to compensate for the missing meat flavor by overfeeding unlucky vegetarians. Thankfully, the chef at Chestnut does not suffer from this lack of confidence. The only entrée under the heading "veg" (one of the pastas is also vegetarian) was the best dish we ate all night. Zucchini "ribbons" were slippery and maintained their crunch buried beneath the "piperade"—a Basque name for a succulent sauté of onions, tomatoes and green peppers. The dish also contained small cubes of ricotta salata and pepitas, both welcome salty textural additions to the plate.

Other menu items are similarly thoughtful and delicate. The salads are composed and tasty, with classic texture and flavor pairings like beets and ginger, tomato and feta and radish and blue cheese. The sockeye salmon with leeks, peas, ramps and garlic is light and delicious with the heft of the dish coming from the onion family rather than butter. The small plates tempted us from the menu but were a little disappointing in execution. The calamari, grilled and stuffed with quinoa, romesco and radish, was flavorless, and the quinoa was overcooked. Their potato gnocchi was sautéed, which may be the preferred cooking method for those not sure of the texture of their gnocchi.

For some, dishes at Chestnut may be undersalted. The flavors are there but not always fleshed out with intense heat or seasoning—except the vegetables. Whether in the salads, the sides, the vegetarian entrée, or accompanying a protein, the vegetables are the best items on the menu at Chestnut. Carnivores may have to hunt for the tastiest dish on the menu, but vegetarians will find delectable greens everywhere they look.

TALIA BERMAN

Fast food can be healthy, particularly when it comes from Chipotle. As I walked into the casual burrito chain, my eyes immediately directed to the menu boards, where more than one decision awaited me.

CHIPOTLE
Mexican, Fast Food
185 Montague St. (Court & Clinton St.)
Ⓝ Ⓡ ② ③ ④ ⑤
718 243-9109
chipotle.com
Daily: 11am–10pm

Chipotle serves healthy Mexican fare, and while the menu isn't long, it offers a lot of options; the contents of the burritos, tacos, salads and burrito bowls (burritos sans the tortilla) are each customizable. Meat options include barbacoa, braised carnitas and adobo-marinated and grilled chicken or steak. Momofuku's David Chang even attempted (unsuccessfully) to work at Chipotle in hopes of unearthing the restaurant's pork recipe. As you make your way down the line, customize your order by choosing from four types of salsas, two preparations of beans and more. Vegetarians, note that the pinto beans are cooked with a small amount of bacon, but the black beans are vegetarian.

My adobo-marinated chicken burrito was well-spiced and fresh, and after all was said and done, with the addition of all the add-ins including cilantro-lime rice, salsa, vegetarian black beans and more, my burrito was about the size of a large brick, more than enough to satisfy a hungry adult. If you're going to get a side of chips, splurge on the guac, which proves to be quite tasty.

Not only is Chipotle delicious and healthy, it also has a conscience about it. The chain's commitment to food integrity means sourcing local and organic produce as much as possible, and using synthetic hormone-free dairy products and meat from animals raised sans antibiotics or added hormones.

Be sure to stop by the utensil stand for some lime wedges to juice up your tacos or guac. Grab a table, dig in and let Chipotle make your conscience feel as good as your taste buds will.   AMY SUNG

COLONIE
New American
127 Atlantic Ave. (Henry & Clinton St.)
② ③ ④ ⑤ Ⓝ Ⓡ
718 855-7500
colonienyc.com
Mon–Wed: 6pm–10:30pm
Thu–Fri: 6pm–11:30pm
Sat: 11am–3pm, 5pm–11:30pm
Sun: 11am–3pm, 5pm–10:30pm

In a borough inundated by rustic-clean décor, Colonie is uniquely impeccable. Under high rough-hewn ceilings, a thriving herb wall divides the brick-walled space. Curious drinkers and diners forgo tables in favor of a spot at the bar up front or open kitchen in back.

Paper placemats play double duty as menus, divvying up the restaurant's sharing-friendly farm-to-table eats into sections like "vegetables" and "crostini." Our crostini pick was a perfect split; mild house ricotta, honey and mint topped two slices of buttery grilled bread. The versatile cheese takes on several roles through the menu, once as thinly sliced ricotta salata on a bright line of heirloom tomatoes. It's the gnudi, however, that will have you waxing poetic about the stuff. Bound by an impossibly thin layer of flour, creamy ricotta found acidic contrast in bursts of warm, sweet cherry tomatoes. Chopped, dehydrated olives added depth to the ethereal dumplings without over salting.

Don't miss "the Egg," where a subtly vinegar-sweet farro with hon shimeji mushrooms and fava beans gets a welcome coating from the fried egg's runny yolk. I was equally fascinated by the grilled escarole, a smoky alternative to your classic greens with padron peppers and a sprinkling of bottarga (dried mullet flakes).

Sustainable fish and meats star in the large plates, from sumptuous scallops made spicy-tart by apricot and curry to a light, satiating fluke with house-made ramp capers, parsley and roasted fingerling potatoes. Carnivores will delight in the skirt steak, whose charred skin—nearly as crispy as the accompanying fries but juicy tender within—gentle garlic aioli and side of watercress kept the dish satisfyingly simple.

From its fall 2010 Kickstarter campaign to its February 2011 launch, this Brooklyn Heights hangout has come a long way. If the local following and locally-sourced eats are any indication, it's moving in the right direction. JACLYN EINIS

First it was the flickering candles in antique holders. Then there were the hanging copper pots, the wooden handcrafted tables, the woven high-back chairs. It is obvious that in Convivium Osteria you are in the hands of Mediterraneans who have mastered two things: creating a romantic space and delivering the

CONVIVIUM OSTERIA
Italian
68 5th Ave. (Bergen St. & St. Marks Pl.)

Ⓓ Ⓝ Ⓡ ② ③

718 857-1833
convivium-osteria.com
Mon–Thu: 6pm–11pm
Fri–Sat: 5:30pm–11:30pm
Sun: 5pm–10pm

clean flavors of Italy, Spain and Portugal. In this Park Slope restaurant chef-owners Carlo and Michelle Pulixi focus on old-world culinary traditions using the finest naturally-raised meat and local, organic produce. This devotion to dishes that allow pure ingredients to shine was evident from the first plate to hit our table: an organic arugula and endive salad, finished with long shavings of parmigiano. Lightly dressed and farm fresh, ingredients this good speak for themselves equally in the creamy buffalo mozzarella and heirloom tomato salad, topped with fragrant basil leaves still on the stem. A pan roasted quail appetizer, with dry figs and port wine reduction, seduced the senses with its slightly sweet aroma and tender meat. Entrées were a lesson of nuances present in the best Mediterranean cooking. On first glance, a red snapper fillet with capers, fresh tomatoes, olives and swiss chard might seem straightforward—but this delicate dish showed respect for the medley of vegetables, no one taste overpowering the others. The Mediterranean might be known for simplicity, but this chef nudges beyond the traditional to craft memorable morsels, such as green apple and cinnamon ravioli with duck ragu, topped with colorful radicchio shavings. A roasted pine nut crusted rack of lamb showcased the gamey character of the meat along with the signature flavor of Portugal, a port wine sauce. A love is present at these tables—for the rustic charm, clean flavors and romance of the Mediterranean.   JESSICA COLLEY

CORNERSTONE
American
271 Adelphi St. (@ Dekalb Ave.)
Ⓐ Ⓒ Ⓖ

718 643-4216
thebrooklyncornerstone.com
Mon–Wed: 11am–11pm
Thu: 11am–12am
Fri: 11am–1am
Sat: 10am–1am
Sun: 10am–11pm

A meathead and a vegetarian walk into a bar.

She digs into a plate of bourbon 'chicken.' He gets busy with a sirloin strip. As he wipes the juice from his mouth, he notices she's giving him the look. "Nah, it's cool baby. It's hormone-free." They feed each other bites of grilled fennel and retire to the more intimate, upstairs bar for a movie and a nightcap. A laid-back sports pub, seasonal comfort food lounge and jazz brunch hangout, Fort Greene's newest Cornerstone is as eclectic as the neighborhood it calls home.

Cornerstone uses all fresh and local vegetables—organic whenever available—so I was disappointed that the starter veggie tower was fried top to bottom. For those seeking meatless comfort, Cornerstone delivers with soy soul 'chicken' nuggets that actually taste like the real thing. However, fried panko flakes aren't so comfy for the heart. Healthy vegetarians may find more solace in a grilled mango "chicken" salad or platter.

Carnivores have plenty of local, organic meats and sustainable seafood to choose from. The flavorful warm spinach salad makes for a solid starter to split. Swine-ophiles may disagree, but I'd like to see the chef add a few more bites of spinach and cut down on the portion and char of the pork belly strips (in both cases, a touch too much of a good thing). The short ribs paired grass-fed smoky beef, red-wine-braised to sweet tenderness, with a side of mildly gingered bok choy and potato gratin. Equally generous, the seasonal grilled yellowfin tuna and asparagus with asparagus-quinoa salad was satisfying and refreshingly light.

Unpretentious, well balanced dishes with seasonal flavors make Cornerstone an omnivore's delight. With wraparound street side dining and an upstairs patio, for those looking to dine healthfully and al fresco: this is your corner.

JACLYN EINIS

100

Diner might have the least traditional "health" food in Brooklyn.

The kale salad bravely comprises whole leaves of kale (instead of the ubiquitous julienned-to-death slivers) with slices of cucumber, radish, pickled green tomatoes and crumbles of feta cheese, all in balance and in season, and would've been perfect if it hadn't

DINER
New American
85 Broadway Ave. (@ Berry St.)

Ⓙ Ⓜ Ⓩ

718 486-3077
dinernyc.com
Mon–Thu: 11am–5pm, 6pm–12am
Fri: 11am–5pm, 6pm–1am
Sat: 10am–4pm, 6pm–1am
Sun: 10am–4pm, 6pm–12am

been drenched by a very unsubtle horseradish-buttermilk dressing. Yes, raw preparations of kale, radish and fennel need something to balance their intense flavors and textures, but an eye for an eye makes the whole world...you know. Better to let the vegetables shine on their own—pickled in lemon juice or even horseradish if you insist.

The buttermilk attack on the kale salad is representative of much of the food at Diner. The famous grass-fed beef burger is formed gently and cooked medium rare, would have been perfect had we not thoughtlessly agreed when our waitress offered, "Cheese?" The cheese was so sharp it overwhelmed the delicate simplicity of the burger.

Diner sources most of their ingredients locally, and the menu changes nightly. The brined half-chicken with ginger-glazed carrots was well-executed and tasty if, again, over-sauced. Try also the fish preparations. Our bonito was tasty, boosted by a sweet carrot puree and pickled vegetable salad.

Though it feels very trendy and somehow impromptu, Diner has been open for 13 years. They don't even print menus; your server writes it on the paper tablecloth as he or she speaks, and then leaves you helpless to remember what was said or to read what was (illegibly) written. Arrive hungry, and don't try to know exactly what you are ordering—the menu "delivery" makes that almost impossible. But the food is good. The peas pop open in your mouth, and proteins are well prepared, so come hungry and enjoy the conscious indulgences.   TALIA BERMAN

EAT
New American
124 Meserole Ave. (@ Leonard St.)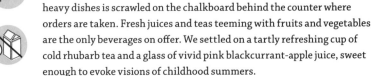
718 389-8083
eatgreenpoint.com
Tue–Sun: 12pm–10pm

Any lingering doubts about the quality of fresh, locally sourced ingredients will be dispelled after a meal at Eat. The humble lunch and dinner spot in Greenpoint puts out some of the most flavorful dishes we've tasted in Brooklyn, all made with seasonal local produce and served on pottery handmade in an on-site kiln.

Dark wood communal tables fill the narrow dining room, and meals are dependent on what's available; every few days or so, a new list of vegetable-heavy dishes is scrawled on the chalkboard behind the counter where orders are taken. Fresh juices and teas teeming with fruits and vegetables are the only beverages on offer. We settled on a tartly refreshing cup of cold rhubarb tea and a glass of vivid pink blackcurrant-apple juice, sweet enough to evoke visions of childhood summers.

Our starters were likewise fresh, fragrant and colorful. A cold carrot soup had a touch of fennel and savory basil to cut through the sweetness of the main ingredient; although slightly warm, the gossamer-weight broth and subtle texture made for a perfectly summery soup. A gorgeously hued salad of pink and red beets with Pawlet cheese (an aged cow's milk variety) and raw shaved fennel was nearly too pretty to eat. A few bites in, however, and we were eagerly devouring the combination of flavors—sweet beets and aromatic fennel—and textures—creamy slices of cheese, mingling with firm, crunchy vegetables. A generous green salad tossed with smoked trout, fresh goat cheese and sliced cucumber arrived next. The cucumber lent crunch to supple green leaf lettuce, slightly smoky and deliciously oily from the pink trout and creamy goat cheese. Our favorite dish of the night followed: summer squash ratatouille with freekah (a nutty grain, similar to barley), spicy green pepper, fennel, cippollini onions, sweet yellow corn and oyster mushrooms. Ratatouille is too often a hastily prepared hodgepodge, but this spicy-sweet bowl was carefully composed, preserving each vegetable's texture and flavor. It was a fitting end to a meal at Eat, where the level of respect for bold, seasonal ingredients is as impressive as the food itself.   SARAH AMANDOLARE

Egg is always busy. My grandmother says, "You can't fool people." Therefore, Egg must be pretty good. And it is. The grilled cheddar cheese on crunchy whole wheat is simply griddled and delicious. Speaking of simple, the simple salad, with mesclun, beets, pecans and a grapefruit vinaigrette, is exactly what it sounds like: bountiful and tasty. The sautéed kale is excellent—firm, juicy, flavorful: kale at its best. Other, more complex preparations, are less successful: the fried chicken is greasy and over-battered, served with bland collard greens, and the dish's only redeeming quality: a perfectly steaming house-made biscuit. The pulled pork sandwich was positively burnt and missing the menu's promise of a vinegar-pepper sauce. Apart from the kale, the vegetarian side dishes disappoint: the lima bean salad is neither hearty nor toothsome (like a good bean should be), slightly over-cooked and otherwise unremarkable. Ditto for the broiled tomatoes, unfortunately accompanying more than one menu item.

Partly responsible for Egg's success: its active role in the community. Egg's owners host dinners to raise money for the Automotive High School Garden on Bedford Avenue, contribute to the Greenpoint Reformed Church Soup Kitchen, and have helped raise money for BK Farmyards, an organization that converts under-utilized urban land to miniature farms. Egg has its own farm in Oak Hill, New York, where they cultivate over 11 acres of land to grow some of what they put on their tables in Williamsburg and educate community members on the importance of sustainability in agriculture. The restaurant itself feels like a neighborhood establishment, with families and hipsters convening in pursuit of a decent meal, good conversation and a chance to feel like part of something bigger than themselves. And if you stick to the simple, seasonal menu items, that is exactly what you will get.

TALIA BERMAN

EGG
American
135 N. 5th St.
(Bedford Ave. & Berry St.) **L**
718 302-5151
pigandegg.com
Mon–Wed: 7am–6pm
Thu: 7am–10pm
Fri: 7am–11pm
Sat: 9am–11pm
Sun: 9am–9pm
(Cash Only)

ELIA

Greek

8611 3rd Ave. (86th & 87th St.) Ⓡ
718 748-9891
eliarestaurant.com
Tue–Thu: 5pm–10pm
Fri–Sat: 5pm–11pm
Sun: 4pm–9pm

Walking into Elia off the bustling 3rd Ave, you feel like you've walked right into Greece. Calming white walls, large archways, rustic wooden ceiling planks, blue wooden shutters and pictures of scenic landscapes paint the picture for this casual fine dining experience.

Pete and Christina Lekkas (also of Purbird in Park Slope) go Greek in Elia's menu, incorporating local produce in select dishes and features proteins like lamb, grass-fed filet mignon and Alaskan salmon. We began our meal with the Marouli and Roca Salata, a salad with shredded romaine, local baby arugula from New Jersey, aged kefalotyri cheese, roasted almonds, yogurt feta dressing and house-made pita croutons. Well dressed, chopped and mixed, it was basically a Greek version of caesar salad. The tiny pita croutons added a welcome crunch.

While tasty warm bread, olive oil and olives are complimentary, a must-try is the appetizer of spreads, which comes with six fresh and flavorful spreads and dips including extremely refreshing tzatziki, htipiti, a feta spread with red pepper and chili, and more, plus a little basket of perfectly thin pita triangles.

The grilled sea bass with tomatoes, olives, fingerling potatoes, young beet greens and onions was cooked to perfection. Fresh tomatoes were stewed to an aromatic and velvety consistency and perfectly supported by the onions and young beet greens, making this dish my favorite of the night, along with the salad and dips. Red and green olives halves sit pretty amidst the blackened fish. This dish was homey, vibrant and fresh, hitting all of the right taste buds with each bite.

Travel to Elia for a trip to Greece with delicious, authentic food, a romantic-yet-casual atmosphere and attentive and friendly service—all without boarding a plane.   AMY SUNG

An organic menu, biodegradable take-away containers and minimalist wood interior set Ella Café apart on restaurant-laden Bedford Avenue in Williamsburg. Former Gramercy Tavern chef Oleg Lyaskoronskiy prefers clean and simple preparations of high quality ingredients, letting natural flavors speak for themselves. Proteins tend to be grilled or roasted, lightly seasoned with fresh herbs and accompanied by seasonal vegetables. Fruits also figure prominently at Ella Café in blended organic juices and smoothies touting vitamin-packed citrus fruits, antioxidant-rich berries and appealing add-ins like ginger, beets and soymilk.

ELLA CAFÉ
American
177 Bedford Ave.
(N. 7th & N. 8th St.) Ⓛ
718 218-8079
ellacafe.com
Mon–Thu: 8am–10pm
Friday: 8am–11:30pm
Sat: 9am–11:30pm
Sun: 10am–10pm

Although tempted by the café's all-day breakfast items like veggie-filled omelets and pancakes with fruit compote, we couldn't resist the array of creative sandwiches, salads and entrées (including several vegetarian and vegan options). We dug into a generous portobello sandwich stacked with roasted red peppers and thick slices of eggplant on soft ciabatta bread. Subtle caper mayo and oozing melted brie completed the deliciously messy sandwich—a bit tricky to bite with all the toppings but worth the struggle. Easier to eat was a Mediterranean salad featuring firm lentils with diced red onion, kalamata olives, amazingly sweet tomatoes and a dollop of rich goat cheese. Arugula leaves and artfully arranged cucumber slices brightened the energizing, protein-packed salad. Impressively, the café prepares its own mesclun salad—a mix of tender arugula, spinach, radicchio and green leaf lettuce. We were similarly pleased with the healthfulness and flavor of our entrée, a grilled flaky filet of fresh-caught tilapia that was stunningly white and moist. We found the accompanying grilled asparagus a touch undercooked but easily polished off the side of ratatouille, which combined savory bay leaf with sweetness from stewed onions and carrots and meaty chunks of eggplant and zucchini. Although understated, such dishes are carefully considered, skillfully prepared and memorably flavorful. We'll be back for breakfast soon.

SARAH AMANDOLARE

THE FARM ON ADDERLEY

New American

1108 Cortelyou Rd. (@ Stratford Rd.)

B Q

718 287-3101
thefarmonadderley.com
Mon–Thu: 9am–3pm, 5:30pm–11pm
Fri: 9am–3pm, 5:30pm–11:30pm
Sat: 10:30am–3pm, 5:30pm–11:30pm
Sun: 10:30am–3pm, 5:30pm–11pm

Around the corner from tree-lined streets with Victorian homes and… driveways, I spotted a family of eight smiling through a windowed storefront. I was not in Manhattan anymore.

Where had the Q taken me? To Ditmas Park, where the Brady Bunch-lookalikes were dining at The Farm on Adderley. Inside, Cortelyou Road's country chic cornerstone was abuzz with diners hungry for a table or seat at the long wooden bar.

The hostess led us through the (minimalist but warm) space to the back dining room, where the works of local artists added a bit of intrigue to brick walls. On a drier night, I would opt for the sweet garden out back.

Dressed the prairie part in flannel and pigtails, our waitress enthusiastically helped us narrow down our wish list from the seasonal, sustainable menu (they list most purveyors on their website). We eased in with a tasty salad of shredded kale with radish, olive oil, lemon and a hefty dose of salty parmesan crumble. Cubes of lemongrass aspic added a foreign twist to an otherwise uncomplicated fruit salad; they melted with the touch of a fork into the sunny mix of watermelons, honeydew, heirloom tomatoes and cucumbers.

Sautéed escarole, onion and sugar snap peas topped a chili-heavy mackerel escabeche. While it strayed from the light and simple flavor expectations "The Farm" may illicit, I enjoyed the delicious play of sweet and spicy kicking around on my tongue. A not-to-be-missed pasture-raised burger was cooked to juicy perfection. Served on a sturdy English muffin, it came with a pickle and delectable fries—both house-made—with an addictive curry mayo for dipping (or spicing up your patty).

As I washed it all down with a harmonious glass of cucumber vodka lemonade (house-made, naturally), I was happy to know The Farm's not far from home.

JACLYN EINIS

Fatty 'Cue takes an innovative approach to barbeque without losing the essence of each ingredient. Dishes at the cubby-sized South Williamsburg spot have Southeast Asian flair, resulting in a slew of potent tastes and mouthwatering aromas. Smoky

FATTY 'CUE
Asian Fusion, Barbeque
91 S. 6th St. (Bedford Ave. & Berry St.)
Ⓙ Ⓜ Ⓩ
718 599-3090
fattycue.com
Daily: 12pm–4pm, 5pm–12am

meats feature naturally sweet glazes and fall tenderly off the bone, while sides tout fresh seasonal produce prepared with Thai and Vietnamese spices and oils.

At our table in the cozy outdoor garden, a knowledgeable waiter crouched down to discuss the menu and daily specials. We ordered a light and crunchy salad of sliced celery dressed in sesame oil; yuzu, a tart citrus fruit, and Tianjin preserved cabbage (a Thai method using salt and garlic) completed the summery dish. Next came fresh milk cheese, which tasted appropriately fresh but had a creamy, lumpy texture we couldn't get used to—we appreciate that Fatty 'Cue is out to challenge palates, though.

There was nothing not to like about the entrées, however. Thanks to our helpful server's suggestion, we dug into a plate piled high with heritage pork ribs. The meat glistened with a sweet-and-tangy-fish-palm glaze so tasty that even the "vegetarian" at our table couldn't resist a few bites. A halved, smoked 'Bobo' chicken arrived next, juicy and flavorful alongside a mellow garlic and peanut dipping sauce. We paired it with decadent, caramel-flavored fingerling potatoes doused in crab butter and finished with sea salt and coarse cracked black pepper. The last dish of the evening was our favorite: rich, tender pieces of lamb shoulder paired with a creamy, garlicky goat yogurt sauce and warm, slightly charred house-made pita. Fatty 'Cue is a place where getting your hands dirty is not up for debate, so dig in, devour your dishes and be grateful to the pitmasters behind the scenes.   SARAH AMANDOLARE

FIVE LEAVES
New American
18 Bedford Ave.
(Lorimer St. & Nassau Ave.)
718 383-5345
fiveleavesny.com
Daily: 8am–1am

Five Leaves has mastered the art of the first impression: charming outdoor tables, a corner location, the unusual 20s era boiler-room door to the WC. When finally getting a table at this no-reservations restaurant in Greenpoint (be prepared to wait at peak times) I wasn't bothered by my neglected stomach, as the list of enticing, healthy dishes seemed worth the wait. The concept here is often called Australian comfort food, and if you can deal with spotty service, there is much to be enjoyed.

Our meal began with the black kale salad, energized with spicy anchovy dressing. While I wanted to keep this salad—finessed with aged gouda and hazelnuts—to myself, appetizers at Five Leaves are portioned to share. One specialty: the house-made ricotta, topped with fresh figs, thyme, honeycomb, maldon sea salt, served with warm fruit-nut bread. A few bites of this dish will satisfy any craving for something creamy. Next came a whole rainbow trout, grilled with lemon and garlic, presented rustically over a bed of fregola, sweet corn and baby bok choy. While tasty, watch out for hunks of raw garlic stuffed into the trout that don't roast as nicely as the white, fleshy fish. Diners with hearty appetites will be drawn to the organic lamb shepherd's pie, served bubbling and topped with honey-roasted root vegetables. While the food concept is clearly defined, the service at times is lost. Multiple servers tended my table, but none claimed responsibility for our comfort. It is a sad end to a lovely evening to have to ask multiple times for the check while watching servers socialize.

The attraction with Five Leaves is first and foremost the warm atmosphere and people watching, second the accomplished food. This restaurant makes a strong case that Australians know their comfort food.
JESSICA COLLEY

Flatbush Farm's outdoor backyard garden dining area is beautiful. It belongs in a fairytale. The indoor dining room is classy and comfortable with strategic wall lighting and 19th century furniture, but sit outside if you can (and you often can, since it is enormous). High trestle walls encompass a vast outdoor dining space that feels simultaneously

FLATBUSH FARM
New American
76 St. Marks Ave. (@ Flatbush Ave.)
Ⓑ Ⓠ ② ③

718 622-3276
flatbushfarm.com
Mon–Thu: 11:30am–3pm, 5:30pm–11pm
Fri: 11:30am–3pm, 5:30pm–12am
Sat: 10:30am–3pm, 5:30pm–12am
Sun: 10:30am–3pm, 5:30pm–11pm

intimate and like being at a great party. Anything would taste good there.

Most of it does. The heirloom bean salad is great, and it is a true vegetarian entrée—a generous scoop of heirloom beans served with roasted peppers, tomato, corn and creamy polenta. Also delicious is the grass-fed hanger steak they often offer as their nightly beef option, simply grilled and heartily seasoned. Definitely opt for the Flatbush bread appetizer, served with Mediterranean-inspired purees and tapenades. The corn cake appetizer, recommended by both bartender and server, was incredibly rich and felt more apt as a hangover cure than a dinner appetizer.

The restaurant is definitely a must-go for the Brooklyn hipster contingent and is very much a Park Slope standby with a growing roster of community events and partnerships (and an increasingly popular brunch starring a delicious (if messy) reuben sandwich called the "Rick Rubin"). Indeed, none of the food is very refined or aesthetically minded. Dishes seem to comprise ingredients either piled or strewn across the plate instead of thoughtfully created and composed.

Flatbush Farm is good for large groups and parties. The menu has something for everyone, there is a sister bar cleverly called, "Bar(n)" next door for before or after, and the staff is more than happy to help you celebrate.   **TALIA BERMAN**

FRAGOLE
Italian
394 Court St.
(1st Pl. & Carroll St.) F G
718 522-7133
fragoleny.com
Mon–Tue: 4pm–11pm
Wed–Sun: 12pm–11pm

Fragole is Italian for "strawberry," but there's no fruit in sight at this homey spot. The brick-walled, intimate trattoria offers a menu packed with straightforward (in a good way) classics.

Though the designation only appears with the menu's many beef dishes, our waiter assured me that nearly everything is, in fact, organically grown. "The owner thinks it tastes better," he said proudly. And he's right, in most cases; the grilled polenta appetizer, a substantial plank smothered in creamy wild mushrooms, looked heavy but was surprisingly delicate: the polenta fluffy and mild, the fontina sauce light enough to support—but not drowned—the funghi. A plate of fresh pappardelle topped with a short rib ragu was the hit of the night, rich and satisfying without being greasy—no easy feat with such a fatty cut of meat. The Black Angus sirloin, lightly daubed with a balsamic glaze, was flavorful and so tender it scarcely needed chewing. Crunchy, mahogany-toned roasted potatoes served alongside added a lovely textural contrast.

However, some of the more vegetable-centric dishes didn't shine so brightly. The Insalata Rustica's sweet, juicy roasted peppers, house-marinated artichoke hearts and pillows of imported mozzarella di bufala were let down by their bed of indifferently-dressed salad mix and bland, cottony tomatoes (especially disappointing at a time of year when there's a gorgeous, ruby-red tomato on every street corner). And the Spaghetti del Pastore, whose description implied a new spin on Pasta Primavera, was downright bland (shocking, considering it featured leeks, garlic, grape tomatoes, artichokes and saffron—but all were buried in a blizzard of ricotta salata).

As a neighborhood Italian restaurant, Fragole is solid—and solidly popular, with every table taken by 7:00. As an Italian restaurant dedicated to organically-grown food, Fragole is ripe for the picking.

DEBBIE KOENIG

Frankies 457 is genius. The menu is long and varied, with salads, sandwiches, crostini, pastas, vegetable plates, cheese and charcuterie—but almost every item on the menu is made from carefully chosen, delicious ingredients that can be prepared in advance and assembled to order. The roasted vegetable salad is a rotating roster of vegetables found in the green markets. Those same vegetables will show up on daily crostini and as garnishes on Antipasti. Frankies must buy pine nuts, ricotta, bacon, arugula and polenta in serious bulk to support the preponderance of these ingredients on the menu. But it is all to a great end—the food tastes fantastic. Preparations are usually two or maybe three ingredients that tango texture and flavor to impressive result.

FRANKIES 457
Italian
457 Court St.
(4th Pl. & Luquer St.) Ⓕ Ⓖ
718 403-0033
frankiesspuntino.com
Sun–Thu: 11am–11pm
Fri–Sat: 11am–12am
(Cash Only)

The roasted beets and avocados with balsamic vinegar are among the best versions available in the city. The two vegetables are perfectly paired—the fatty avocado and the sweet beets enrich each other, and both are cut by the acid in the balsamic vinegar. Mentionable vegetable antipasti are the cauliflowers, roasted carrots and hot pine nut polenta. The first two are simple and roasted to a fleshy perfection, and the incredibly rich polenta is still lovely and pillowy, accented by a soft bite from the pine nuts. From the pasta menu, the house-made gnocchi with fresh marinara is large and straightforward, while the sweet potato and sage ravioli is tangy and flavorful.

Frankies 457 is the first restaurant from Frank Castronovo and Frank Falcinelli, owners of Frankies Spuntino in Manhattan, Prime Meats down the street and Pedlar coffee shops. From the street Frankies doesn't look like much, but the outside walkway leads to a huge rustic dining room with high ceilings and wood paneling… when combined with the food, it's truly magical dining.   TALIA BERMAN

FRANNY'S
Italian
295 Flatbush Ave.
(Prospect Pl. & St. Marks Ave.)
② ③ ④ Ⓑ Ⓠ
718 230-0221
frannysbrooklyn.com
Mon–Thu: 5:30pm–11pm
Fri: 5:30pm–11:30pm
Sat: 12pm–11:30pm
Sun: 12pm–11pm

It is not easy to standout in a city brimming with gourmet pizza restaurants, but Franny's has figured out how to do it.

First, acknowledge your vendors and purveyors by printing their names and contributions on the back of your menu. Thank Eckerton Hill Farms for the hot peppers they grow so the white pizza with ricotta and buffalo mozzarella will be properly spicy. Assure your guests

that Counter Culture Coffee will provide certified fair-trade and shade-grown coffee, and make mention of Tri-State Biodiesel, who converts Franny's kitchen grease to biodiesel fuel.

Second, champion unfailingly simple flavor combinations: fried green tomatoes with ramp and anchovy mayonnaise, mezze maniche (a thicker, more rustic version of penne) with zucchini, mint and parmigiano reggiano.

Third, treat waiting guests (you almost always have to wait to dine) with forthrightness, quoting actual wait times and making real suggestions about other places to go when dining at Franny's isn't going to happen for them.

Simple dishes are the best. Start with the Marinated Greens with Aldo Armato extra virgin olive oil, a generous portion that includes fennel fronds and actually tastes "marinated"—like the oil has had some time to integrate its flavor into the spicy greens. The pizzas are uniformly excellent, each one thoughtfully crafted and smartly executed with a perfectly rustic crust. A lot of guests seem annoyed that they have to cut their own pizza, but to me, it came as a welcome interaction with the fantastic food.   TALIA BERMAN

It is possible to make high quality accessible.

The General Greene, a quiet and casual Fort Greene eatery, offers dressed-down complexity and depth from the thoughtfully sourced menu to the outdoor organic ice cream stand, to the adjoining grocery store offering local, handcrafted products and prepared foods. Deceptively simple classics like roast chicken and burgers with subtly flavorful sauces, free range and antibiotic-free meat, and house-made specialty toppings fill the menu. While the kitchen is putting out high quality food, the restaurant is firmly down-to-earth; soft wood, muted tones and relaxed waitstaff ensure a comforting meal. We eased into our dinner with two small plates, both of which turned out to be unusually small—if you're famished, order a couple per person— and uncommonly delicious. Organic wild rice salad was toothsome and firm, with small chunks of mellow golden beets, bitter radicchio leaves to set off sweet pickled shallots, and a light mustard vinaigrette marrying it all. Between bites of rice, we nibbled on garlicky sautéed kale with just enough chili heat and fresh lemon to make it memorable.

Plates are served whenever they're ready, making for a leisurely paced experience, and our 100 percent grass-fed, antibiotic-and-hormone-free beef burger arrived piping hot. We appreciated the soft, charmingly unadorned bun and traditional toppings, like sweet house-made bread-and-butter pickles and red onion slices. Fresh mixed greens and thin, crispy fries accompanied the burger, which was followed by a juicy half-chicken cooked under a brick. The Giannone antibiotic-free bird sat in a rosemary shallot sauce so light and fragrant that we found ourselves spooning it up and eating on its own. These seemingly little things— carefully prepared sauces, addictive house-made add-ons and flavorful finishing touches—are what The General Greene does best. The end result is a restaurant that makes a big impression.   SARAH AMANDOLARE

THE GENERAL GREENE
New American
229 Dekalb Ave. (@ Clermont St.) G
718 222-1510
thegeneralgreene.com
Mon–Fri: 8am–11pm
Sat: 9am–11pm
Sun: 9am–10pm

THE GROCERY
New American
288 Smith St.
(Sackett & Union St.)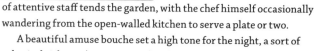
718 596-3335
thegroceryrestaurant.com
Tue–Thu: 5:30pm–10pm
Fri: 5:30pm–11pm
Sat: 5pm–11pm

The Grocery brings understated elegance to the ground floor of a Carroll Gardens townhouse and an extra touch of sophistication to seasonal dining. Glide through the grey-green dining room to the tabelclothed patio, where Brooklyn's eco-minded well-to-do dine amidst tall pines and lights strung along picket fences. A host of attentive staff tends the garden, with the chef himself occasionally wandering from the open-walled kitchen to serve a plate or two.

A beautiful amuse bouche set a high tone for the night, a sort of spherical rich man's tater tot with a shot of creamy-sweet corn soup. We took advantage of the kitchen's abundance of fresh produce by ordering a small serving of "vegetables" (the large could be a meal all its own). The market plate featured a smorgasbord of greens, grains and legumes, including several citrusy forkfuls of wheat berries and sautéed green beans which (for better or worse) seemed untouched by anything but water. Our request for beets prompted the creation of a beet side plate, little red cubes topping paper thin circles of golden beets.

Radishes packed greater flavor, served with slightly salty-bitter mix of Greek feta, red mustard, corona beans and white anchovy vinaigrette. The broiled haddock was surrounded by favas, English peas and a just-salty-enough salt cod-potato dumpling in a light leek and spring onion sauce. A slow rendered duck breast elevated the uber-tender meat with chewy buckwheat groats, garlic-chili broccoli rabe and caramelized red wine sauce.

While The Grocery's à la carte prices send you out of the Gardens and back to Manhattan, I expect their other meats and greens to be equally inspired. Thanks to the affordable tasting menu and green plate special, I'll be back to find out.

JACLYN EINIS

Three-quarters restaurant/café and one quarter frame shop, Healthy Nibbles sits on the busy corner of Flatbush Avenue and Prospect Place, making it a convenient re-fueling stop for the health conscious. In spite of its name, Healthy Nibbles offers much more than just nibbles; in addition to fresh juices and handheld snacks and treats, the menu features wholesome sandwiches, wraps, salads and burgers.

HEALTHY NIBBLES
American, Fast Food
305 Flatbush Ave. (@ Prospect Pl.)
② ③ ④ Ⓑ Ⓠ
718 636-5835
No Website
Mon–Sat: 10am–8pm
Sun: 10am–6pm

A casual and clean atmosphere is complemented by a few quirky and eclectic touches—among them, bright mossy-colored walls and empowering dish names. The counter-service café caters to any type of healthy eater with vegetarian, vegan and meat options.

Healthy Nibbles' "I Am Phenomenal" turkey burger stood out from the standard bird burger with a tangy, slightly spicy and smoky kick (thanks to its house-made ketchup and vegan chipotle mayo). In addition to the flavorful condiments, free-range turkey, organic mixed greens and sautéed red onions sat on the toasted whole wheat bun. It was tasty and perfectly light; we'll be back to try the wild salmon version.

The vegan tofu curry chicken salad sandwich was flavor-packed with plenty of raisins, cumin and other spices. While a little too bitter for me, my dining partner thought it was perfectly seasoned; we both agreed there should have been a disclaimer for the seriously spicy kick.

Jamaican patties from Canarsie are also available in three varieties: vegan soy chicken curry, veggie and chicken curry. While Jared recommends avoiding processed soy proteins, Healthy Nibbles features organic soy and the vegan soy version we tried was surprisingly flavorful and featured a flaky and not-too-greasy crust.

Dessert lovers: conclude your healthy eats with a sugar-free chocolate chip cookie. Whether you're out shopping or just finished yoga, Healthy Nibbles will satiate your appetite in the healthiest way.

AMY SUNG

ICI

New American

246 Dekalb Ave. (@ Vanderbilt Ave.) G

718 789-2778

icirestaurant.com

Mon–Thu: 5:30pm–10pm

Fri: 5:30pm–11pm

Sat: 9am–4pm, 5:30pm–11pm

Sun: 9am–4pm, 5:30pm–10pm

When you order the cucumber and radish salad at iCi, you taste the cucumber and radish. You also taste the French sorrel, Kalamata olives, feta, white anchovies and Thai basil vinaigrette. And somehow, the incredible diversity of flavors doesn't overwhelm the palate; in fact, it tastes good. Even better is the market salad, comprised of greens, slivers of raw sunchoke, and grana padano shavings. The spiced and seared duck breast is another winner, trimmed of fat and served over a meaty ragu of chicory, caramelized baby carrots and wax beans, topped with strips of Meyer lemon zest. The pan-seared wild striped bass, while cooked simply and perfectly, comes with incongruous piles braised baby fennel and sliced summer squash, all sharing a black squid ink vinaigrette that seems there more for visual effect than flavor. Vegetarian-friendly ricotta cavatelli with farm vegetables, corn butter and grana padano is tasty but incredibly rich. Perhaps it would have better if the sauce was made with corn stock and a touch of butter instead of the other way around. Vegetable side dishes are almost meals in themselves: try the marinated red and purple beets with whipped goat cheese, toasted pistachios and mint.

Eating at iCi is like eating in someone's home. The main dining room was maybe the entrance or "great room." The upstairs is a private event space, and there is a magical garden out back; perhaps someone even lived here recently. The décor is strikingly simple, with lots of white votive candles and light-brown wooden table sets. The bathroom is singular, bright white and stocked with fragrant lavender, and the waiting line invites conversation with strangers. "Is that a flank steak that just went by?" a woman asked.

"It must be the hanger," I said.

"I can smell it from here." She said.

"Yum."

TALIA BERMAN

Strolling down a leafy, cobbled street in Brooklyn Heights I wondered how Iris Café could possibly compare to the charm of this quaint neighborhood. Then I saw the sunny storefront, the cozy window seats, the etched ceilings, a relaxed dining room with exposed brick walls. Iris Café matches the neighborhood perfectly—both are a quiet escape from honking horns and bustling streets.

IRIS CAFÉ
New American
20 Columbia Pl. (Joralemon & State St.)
② ③ ④ ⑤ Ⓝ Ⓡ

718 722-7395
iriscafenyc.com
Mon–Fri: 7:30am–5pm
Sat–Sun: 8am–6pm
(Cash Only)

Beyond the welcoming atmosphere, there's the thoughtful food. Orders are made at the counter, so hang back first to read the list of sandwiches, salads and platters on the black chalkboard. My lunch began with the eggplant platter, an enticing mix of roasted eggplant and zucchini, dense hummus topped with a pool of extra virgin olive oil, smooth babaganoush and toasted whole grain bread to scoop it all up. Iris Café has vegetarian options that will tempt even the most ardent meat lovers, such as the rich avocado sandwich. Adorably served only on paper, this sandwich started with two pieces of whole grain bread, filled with slivers of quick pickle, NY state cheddar, lettuce, just-ripe avocado and a sweet note of chutney. Meat options are equally appealing, including the French dip sandwich. This classic roast beef on baguette combination receives a unique upgrade with its coffee-beef jus dipping sauce—I happily dunked the baguette right in. On the lighter side, the cobb salad is a fresh combination of greens, sliced hard-boiled egg, that quick pickle again, crunchy walnuts and blue brie, all topped with shredded herb turkey.

This laid-back location (where no computers are allowed), is also stocked with farm-fresh ingredients available for purchase. Once every morsel of your meal is devoured, pick up some fresh eggs to take home.

JESSICA COLLEY

ISA

New American

348 Wythe Ave. (@ S. 2nd St.) Ⓛ
347 689-3594
isa.gg/isa
Mon–Fri: 11am–4pm, 6pm–11:30pm
Sat–Sun: 10am–4pm, 6pm–11:30pm

Manhattan-based restauranteur Taavo Somer set across the river to open his first solo venture, Isa (meaning "father" in Estonian) in Williamsburg. The gorgeous space feels like an airy, modern barn with a large hearth, exposed kitchen, a wall of logs for the wood-burning stove and doors opening to the street. In a style called "primitive modernism," chef Ignacio Mattos (formerly of Il Buco) executes rustic, seasonal fare with produce hailing from the restaurant's rooftop garden.

The printed daily menu only featured about a dozen dishes (the eatery was still in its soft-launch phase) with minimal descriptions, yet no detail seemed overlooked. Even the trio of freshly baked bread came alongside soft butter dusted with peppercorns and fennel seeds. A start of peppery horseradish shavings awakened our palate and added sharpness to coins of pickled daikon and kombu ribbons, while our Treviso salad tossed with creamy nut cheese and pistachio granola was a much milder appetizer. Adventurous eaters can get their hands dirty with cylinders of chewy, fat-laden pig's tail glazed with chili and garlic (intended to be eaten sans silverware) or try to brave the sardine. Two large, meaty filets sitting in olive oil surround the fish's crisped full skeleton and head—all meant for nibbling. On the refined side, our delicate cod filet performed beautifully when accompanied with silken cauliflower puree, fresh dill flowers and a dollop of tart orange confit. To finish, we blissfully spooned smoked yolk (which came cradled in an egg shell) over sliced rib eye and sweet glazed carrots.

At the time, Isa was BYO (waiting for their liquor license) and cash only, but the knowledgable staff affirmed that change was on the horizon. The vibe here is approachable and friendly, a warm neighborhood spot that I look forward to cozying up to again.

MEGAN MURPHY

The food at Juventino is a little Latino, a little French and a little Italian, but mostly it is American, local, seasonal and fresh. The menu contains "lengua" (tongue) tacos, it contains "velouté" of broccoli (soup), and it contains risotto di farro. While these items may seem to belong in different restaurants, at Juventino they come together in pursuit of a wholesome, bountiful, diversified dining experience that is precisely what you get.

JUVENTINO
New American
370 5th Ave. (5th & 6th St.)
Ⓓ Ⓝ Ⓡ Ⓕ Ⓖ
718 360-8469
juventinonyc.com
Mon–Sat: 10am–4pm, 6pm–10pm
Sun: 10am–4pm

Start with a seasonal salad—a mountain of greens offset by seasonal garnishes that might include squash, or tomatoes, or apples. Then move on to a taco, a great light mid-course or appetizer on offer as a selection of four (or available individually). The hongo (mushroom) tacos are particularly memorable for their chewy, meaty, earthy flavor, offset by a few squeezes of lime, raw onion and corn tortilla.

The best entrée is easily the seared rack of lamb, served with a braised lamb leg tamal, culture-stuffed yogurt squash blossoms and mole poblano. The rack is sliced into chops and seared, meaty and delicious. The tamal, flavored with braising liquid from the lamb leg and peppered with juicy pieces of meat, is a perfect accompaniment to the chops. To cut through the fatty, richness of the lamb, the yogurt-stuffed squash blossoms are fully of racy acidity, only enhanced by mild sweetness in mole poblano.

The vegetarian board is a nice idea, but it is avoidable, since it is mostly just a scoop of sides that accompany each meat dish.

Portions at Juventino are huge. Not just American-portion huge, but widen your eyes and drop your jaw when you see mound upon mound of food huge. Be warned, but don't be deterred—the food is good enough to eat, even in such generous amounts.   TALIA BERMAN

KARLOFF

Eastern European

254 Court St. (@ Kane St.)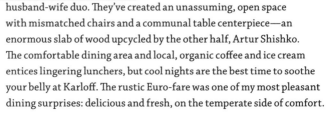
347 689-4279
karloffbrooklyn.com
Mon–Fri: 8am–10pm
Sat–Sun: 9am–10pm

What's sweeter than affordable, "seasonal comfort food" in an uncramped Cobble Hill café? The people behind it. Beside a small, smiley staff, Karloff co-owner Olga Shishko lifts spirits and nourishes bodies with her warm demeanor and home-style Eastern European cooking.

She's one half of Karloff's Russian husband-wife duo. They've created an unassuming, open space with mismatched chairs and a communal table centerpiece—an enormous slab of wood upcycled by the other half, Artur Shishko. The comfortable dining area and local, organic coffee and ice cream entices lingering lunchers, but cool nights are the best time to soothe your belly at Karloff. The rustic Euro-fare was one of my most pleasant dining surprises: delicious and fresh, on the temperate side of comfort.

Seasonal ingredients dictate Karloff's clipboard- and chalkboard-displayed offerings. Washed down perfectly by complimentary cucumber water, our kale and collard greens soup with broccoli puree was like a tasty, slightly bitter split-pea soup. Our big green salad was likewise fresh but less novel. Mesclun mix, hard-boiled egg and a few blasé bites of tomatoes, beets and blueberries were subtly sweet-tarted by a bright grapefruit vinaigrette.

Local, sustainable meats carry the mains, though pescetarians can count on a healthy grilled fish. We dug into two big cabbage rolls, stuffed with ground beef, organic rice and market vegetables and made relatively light by a tomato broth base. Bursting with organic rice and twelve vegetables, the giant stuffed pepper rendered meat altogether superfluous. It sat with carrots and yams in an addictive, yam–sweetened broth.

Karloff's specialty beverages, like organic kefir smoothies, provided alternatives to dessert. We opted for "kampot," a cool, straw-and-spoonworthy sugar-free "soup." Like the rest of the meal, it packed a punch (here, of the fruit variety) without being overly decadent. Few things could be sweeter.

JACLYN EINIS

Central European fare might not be the first food genre that springs to mind for healthy eaters—but a meal at Korzo in Park Slope could change all that. Grass-fed beef is delivered straight from a farm in Ghent, New York (coincidentally also the name of a town in Central Europe), and produce is sourced locally as well.

KORZO
Central European
667 5th Ave. (19th & 20th St.) D N R
718 285-9425
korzorestaurant.com
Mon–Thu: 3pm–11:30pm
Fri: 12pm–11:30pm
Sat–Sun: 11am–11:30pm

At first glance Korzo looks like a cozy neighborhood bar with a range of beers on tap, but there's also a spacious room in the back with plentiful long wooden tables. A clientele of central Europeans craving the tastes of home fill the tables regularly, but this restaurant deserves a wider audience. The pierogi of the day started my Park Slope venture to central Europe. Delightfully chewy organic whole-wheat pierogi were stuffed with tender pulled pork and served on a sophisticated, sculptural plate tossed with tomato and chopped zucchini. A hefty spinach salad came next, each bite revealing fresh ingredients: first, crispy sliced pears, then sweet Muscat grapes, finished sparingly with hunks of blue cheese. On a cold night, few dishes could be as exponentially comforting as the hearty slow-cooked Hungarian goulash. This spicy paprika beef stew was topped with pan-seared spaetzle, caramelized onions and red peppers. The combination of special spices and grass-fed beef had radiant results. Korzo also offers appealing specials on weekdays, including grass-fed burgers on Thursday nights. My juicy organic beef burger was expertly cooked, topped with melty Emmenthaler cheese and a welcome tang from mustard and pickles (both made in-house). Be sure to choose the German Kaiser roll and skip the fried Hungarian bread option. This restaurant delivers precisely what it promises: the nourishing traditions of central European comfort food, always locally sourced. The results are über-delicious.

JESSICA COLLEY

LE BARRICOU
French
533 Grand St.
(Lorimer St. & Union Ave.) Ⓛ Ⓖ
718 782-7372
lebarricouny.com
Mon–Fri: 11am–4pm, 6pm–12am
Sat–Sun: 11am–12am

Williamsburg has seen its fair share of French bistros pop up recently, but Le Barricou charms like no other spot in the neighborhood. Jean-Pierre Marquet's cozy candlelit haunt has a 19th-century ambiance, with dated newspaper clippings plastered on the walls, an elongated wooden bar and vintage accents scattered throughout the rustic interior. A floor-to-ceiling window facade opens to sidewalk seating on Grand Street and an intimate wine lounge displays antique furnishings and a wood burning fireplace. While the décor may be reminiscent of a classic Parisian parlor, the cuisine is far from old-fashioned with a menu featuring refined French fare.

Chef Joab Masse elegantly showcases locally sourced produce and organic, antibiotic- and hormone-free proteins. The signature Le Barricou salad was served with shaved watermelon and thinly sliced radishes, apples and pears over watercress; sweet honey maple vinaigrette and the hot-flavored flesh of spicy black radishes created a striking flavor contrast that I found addicting. Vegetarian options include light house-made ricotta and wild mushroom stuffed ravioli cradled in delicate tomato, garlic and white wine sauce and creamy seasonal vegetable risotto kissed with truffle oil. The night's standout entrée was a tender Creekstone Farms Black Angus hanger steak, massaged with garlic confit and caramelized shallot-red wine jus. Reviews were mixed on the hefty grilled Berkshire pork chop, which arrived crusted with thick anchovy tapenade; unfortunately, the too salty taste (I'm admittedly not an anchovy fan) kept me from enjoying the succulent meat, though my dining companion raved about it. I only wish the menu described how prominent anchovies are in the dish.

The bistro's full bar serves expertly crafted cocktails and exclusively French wines, while the knowledgeable, attentive staff and inviting atmosphere made for a truly delightful dining experience. Merci, Le Barricou.   MEGAN MURPHY

You might have heard about the "Big Salad" at the Lighthouse. "They" say it's huge and delicious and has everything in it—"they" are mostly right. It is huge and delicious; while it doesn't have everything, everything it has, you want. Vegetables are sliced thinly and dressed gently. Avocado and queso fresco are daintily distributed—the perfect treatment for such rich elements. Generously proportioned: the string beans, garbanzo beans, corn and cabbage. The balance is perfect, and the mustard vinaigrette has that missing sweet touch to bring it all together.

THE LIGHTHOUSE
New American
145 Borinquen Pl. (@ Keap St.)
Ⓛ Ⓖ Ⓙ Ⓜ Ⓩ

347 789-7742
lighthousebk.com
Tue–Thu: 6pm–12am
Fri: 6pm–1am
Sat–Sun: 12pm–4pm, 6pm–1am

Other menu items are equally successful. The lamb chops are lean, bursting with flavor and topped with a pungent "salsa verde". The fish of the day was a porgy from Massachusetts, grilled whole and seasoned simply with olive oil, lemon, grilled fennel, memorable baby red onions, grapefruit and a somewhat indistinguishable rhubarb jam.

The Lighthouse touts their raw bar—a daily ceviche, tartare and local oyster selection with a variety of mignonettes and sauces—and they should. The wild striped bass ceviche was light and citrusy while the Spanish mackerel tartare was rich and creamy with sharp chives to cut the richness.

The Israeli-born brother and sister team that own the restaurant allow their native food culture to seep through the menu in spirit rather than in item or style. The kitchen is certainly not afraid of parsley nor garlic. The pungency of aioli and yogurt—so often subdued in American cuisine—shines at the Lighthouse, and the results are wonderful.

Try the menu's "additions": Brussels sprouts with roasted walnuts, apple cider and Valdeón (a Spanish blue cheese), roasted cauliflower with Manchego, olive oil and pine nuts, or simple roasted garlic potatoes with a garlic aioli. They taste like dishes the chef would make for his family; while you're dining, you almost feel as though you are. **TALIA BERMAN**

LILLA CAFÉ
New American
126 Union St.
(Columbia & Hicks St.) Ⓕ Ⓖ
718 855-5700
lillacafe.com
Tue–Wed: 5pm–10pm
Thu–Sun: 11am–4pm, 5pm–10pm

Bringing farm-fresh American cuisine to a traditionally Italian neighborhood, Lilla Café is a charming little eatery in the Columbia Waterfront District. Located right off the BQE, this Union Street gem embraces you with a warm candlelit and exposed brick interior, but don't miss the courtyard garden—a tranquil, green oasis flourishing with fresh herbs that beckons you to dine alfresco from springtime until fall.

Owner-chef Erling Berner focuses on seasonal produce and quality proteins to execute an all-American menu nuanced with Southern, Italian and Latin influences. After settling into an outdoor table, our server presented a basket of house-baked focaccia bread with herb butter while enthusiastically reciting a myriad of tempting market-driven specials. A few minutes later, an appetizer of thick white asparagus spears topped with a perfectly poached egg arrived, followed shortly after by a beautifully balanced salad of sweet watermelon chunks, mild-flavored feta cheese and tangy balsamic vinegar over peppery watercress. Other vegetarian offerings included a velvety asparagus soup and delicate hand-rolled pici pasta tossed with ricotta, zucchini and green beans.

Each meat entrée we sampled was generous in both size and flavor. A thick slab of grilled pork porterhouse was tender and juicy with a red pepper and caper caponata accompaniment, and two hearty pieces of fall-off-the-bone roasted Amish chicken were accompanied by a crisp polenta cake and garlicky broccolini. The succulent seared tri tip steak melted in our mouths, but we wished the mild chimichurri sauce had a bit more of a kick.

Service was genuine and the relaxing atmosphere will make you feel at home—we didn't want to leave. Plus, the restaurant is BYO (and doesn't charge a corkage fee!), so grab your favorite bottle, kick back and the rest will be taken care of. MEGAN MURPHY

Don't expect to order quickly at Locanda Vini e Olii in Clinton Hill—there is too much to admire. From the restored wooden interior of a century-old pharmacy to the Tuscan-inspired menu, everything about this restaurant will captivate your attention. Where medications and potions were once arranged on wooden shelves, generous wine glasses and country-inspired china now grace the walls.

LOCANDA VINI E OLII
Italian
129 Gates Ave. (@ Cambridge Pl.)

718 622-9202
locandany.com
Tue–Thu: 6pm–10:30pm
Fri–Sat: 6pm–11:30pm
Sun: 6pm–10pm

During my visit, I was happily seated at a table for two in the window, perfect for watching the bustle of the restaurant unfold around me. Locanda Vini e Olii has been praised for service that elevates your experience into a personal one. This was confirmed during my meal, as owner Michael Schall worked the floor, revealing his encyclopedic knowledge of ingredients and preparations with a smile. After debating between several appealing options, we sat back at the brown paper-topped table for a parade of rustic dishes.

First came an Italian perspective on salad, combining dried Sicilian figs, gorgonzola, baby lettuce, celery and walnuts into one distinctive bowl. A rush of garden-fresh flavors came next with rich salmon tartare crostini, served three ways over crunchy country-style bread, including bright orange with basil, tangy lemon with mint and grapefruit, dill, and pink peppercorn. The Primi course demonstrated simple flavors as black pepper pici (hand-rolled eggless pasta with black pepper in the dough) was enhanced with roasted onions, grana padano cheese and tarragon. The savory aroma of this dish was satisfying even before the first bite. Italians leave meat for last, when previous courses have tempered the appetite. Expertly grilled duck breast was served sliced and unadorned beyond caramelized sweet onions—a study in the visceral pleasure of serving free-range meat unmasked. Locanda Vini e Olii is perfect for an evening of satiating dishes along with the boisterous laughter of a restaurant with true Italian soul.   JESSICA COLLEY

LODGE
American
318 Grand St. (@ Havemeyer St.)
Ⓙ Ⓜ Ⓩ Ⓛ Ⓖ
718 486-9400
lodgenyc.com
Sun–Thu: 11am–12am
Fri–Sat: 11am–1am

The food and atmosphere at Lodge aim to transport their tattooed and pierced Brooklynites to a humbler and more slow-paced retreat. High wooden ceilings, rows of antlers and a Johnny Cash loop set the country scene and distract diners from their immediate urban surroundings(which include a popular skeeball bar, cigarette-wielding throngs and the hip Paul Frank boutique up the block). Rocking chairs and checkerboards would have proved apt replacements for the scattering of tables both inside and outside the restaurant.

The fare is equally down-to-earth; mild seasoning allows the hormone-free proteins and simple veggie sides to properly assert themselves. A pear and walnut salad is barely coated with vinaigrette but chock-full of its juicy and crunchy namesake ingredients. Salmon is garnished with only salt, pepper and grilled lemon slices, while the grass-fed hanger steak's beefy flavor is also readily discernible beneath very modest adjustments. Luckily, entrées come with their fair share of greens and fruits. The aforementioned salmon and steak are respectfully accompanied by resilient asparagus spears and a refreshing salad of watermelon cubes, fresh mint and feta cheese crumbles. We ordered an extra side of steamed broccoli as well, which arrived sans sauce, spices or dressing like its fellow dishes. For a night of relaxation without leaving behind the trendy, fast-moving backdrop, Lodge offers a straightforward, healthful menu and humble vibe in Brooklyn's most youthful neighborhood.

ALLIX GENESLAW

Self-defined as "a parcel of land located on block 886 in Brooklyn" that "also happens to be a place that serves delicious food," Lot 2 is all about connecting to your environment. They help diners do so through well-priced, wonderfully flavored locavore "lots."

LOT 2
New American

687 6th Ave. (19th & 20th St.)
718 499-5623
lot2restaurant.com
Tue–Sat: 6pm–Close
Sun: 5pm–Close

The space eases with bare bones décor; wood floors, a white ceiling and spare white walls are accented by exposed brick, wooden beams and a strip of chalk scrawled with the night's specials. The casual cool continues with paper wrapping the tables like postage parcels and listing the week's menu in flimsy strips.

"Small lots" had a vegetarian bent, and luckily Lot 2 makes a mean salad. Lemon alone optimized brilliantly fresh arugula, fennel and cherry tomatoes. Pancetta vinaigrette, mint and a lovely goat's milk feta gave roasted beets a nicely salted new dress. However, it was the community-farmed Project EATS summer beans, sautéed and tossed with pine nuts, lemon and ricotta salata, that had us licking our forks (read: fingers).

"Big lots" proved much heartier. The pulled pork was sweetened with honey and barbecue sauce, served alongside a crisp slaw of sliced sweet peppers and not-so-healthy but tasty hush puppies. We enjoyed it, but found baked polenta to be the real treat. It carried a gentle heat—both temperature- and roasted jalapeno-wise—from crusty exterior to soft center. Met by Cayuga black beans, fresh corn, a bit of cheddar, purslane and a fried farm egg, this was comfort food worth leaving your comfort zone for.

Halfway between the Prospect Expressway and Greenwood Cemetery, the restaurant's a bit off the beaten path. And for those who find their way to Block 886, that's a good thing; in a parcel of Williamsburg or West Village land, hungry hordes would leave little room for the relaxed, rural charm that serves the Greenwood Heights lot so well.

JACLYN EINIS

LUNETTA
Italian
116 Smith St. (Dean & Pacific St.)
Ⓐ Ⓒ Ⓕ Ⓖ

718 488-6269
lunetta-ny.com
Sun–Thu: 5:30pm–10pm
Fri–Sat: 5:30pm–11pm

A bit of bell'Italia lives in Boerum Hill thanks to Lunetta, a cozy neighborhood trattoria. Mismatched sconces light Smith Street's "little moon," while classic red banquettes line the walls, and wide counters let diners gaze upon the bar and open kitchen. Out back, a bamboo-bordered garden provides space for 30.

The unfussy, market-driven menu welcomes plate-sharing. I set my sights on one of four bruschette, which proved to be a brilliant start to the meal. House-made leMon– and honey-infused ricotta topped with an essential sprinkling of sea salt on top made a thin slice of sesame-crusted bread sing. A fresh if forgettable salad of roasted beets and dandelion greens came with a creamy, tangy rocchetta cheese crostini (also on sesame-crusted bread).

One of the menu's few seafood items, the tagliarini with wild gulf shrimp, sungold tomatoes and (almost indiscernible) fennel was decent but lacked the flavor to transport you to either sea or farm. More impressive were Lunetta's meatballs with orecchiette (one of several pastas you can add to the dish). Ground walnuts lent the savory meatballs—a mix of Berkshire pork and grass-fed beef—a subtle, appetizing crunch. The toothsome orecchiette made perfect mini cups for sopping up the tasty toasted garlic tomato sauce.

A grass-fed steak looked better than it tasted. Despite promising grill marks and a juicy pink center, it arrived lukewarm and a touch on the tough side. While I enjoyed the tasty porcini rub, the meat itself fell a little flat. The steak came with a gentle salsa verde and roasted fingerling potatoes, but a side dish of grilled summer squash with mint and red pepper gave me the green I needed to round out the meal.

If you're looking for comfort, find it by way of Italian flavors, local ingredients and a relaxing setting at Lunetta.   JACLYN EINIS

Slide though Manhattan Inn's dimly lit, reclaimed-wooden bar to the dining room, a sexy throwback to the days when piano men ruled the lounge. Hungry hipsters fill old movie-theater seats along the lofty room's periphery, moss-adorned lights overhead and a baby grand at center. Local pianists tickle the ivories to the likes of ragtime and New Orleans jazz every night (and for Sunday brunch), as diners sip on new and updated-old-school cocktails.

MANHATTAN INN
New American
632 Manhattan Ave.
(Nassau & Bedford Ave.) **L** **G**
718 383-0885
themanhattaninn.com
Mon–Thu: 6pm–11pm
Fri: 6pm–12am
Sat: 11am–4pm, 6pm–12am
Sun: 11am–4pm, 6pm–11pm

The buzz subsides for bites of New American cuisine. Served with a small side of greens, an unfussy grass-fed grilled hanger steak hit the spot, while a side of roasted Catskills purple potatoes missed the mark. Eager for whole or halved potatoes, I was deflated by thin slices which were aided in spice (but not moisture) by a drizzle of Huancaina sauce. The ceviche brought me back up with generous chunks of scallops sweetened by a floral marinade of mandarin, mint and fennel pollen.

We weren't as enthusiastic about our vegetarian selections. A promising summer pasta didn't quite deliver; the pappardelle, wild mushrooms, grape tomato confit, artichoke puree, fried capers, parmesan and egg never truly synced. Perhaps the sunny side up egg's unrunny yolk was the missing glue needed to bind the elements together. On the simpler side, the grilled cheese was disappointingly devoid of the classic sandwich's crispy-oozy essence. Happily, bright flavors prevailed again in the grilled calamari salad, a tasty mix of arugula, roasted red peppers, feta and crispy capers in orange dressing.

My visit coincided with Manhattan Inn's new menu launch, so I expect all of its dishes will soon be as harmonious as the space is. For now, let the speakeasy vibe seduce you and seasonal preparations sustain you. Stick around for a late-night menu to sate those midnight cravings with organic snacks, live music and DJ sets.   JACLYN EINIS

MARLOW & SONS
New American
81 Broadway Ave. (@ Berry St.)
Ⓛ Ⓙ Ⓜ Ⓩ
718 384-1441
marlowandsons.com
Daily: 8am–4pm, 5pm–12am

Marlow and Sons' menu is very simple. It is one page that also serves as your placemat and contains sections entitled, "Appetizers," "Entrées," "Meat," and "Cheese." The names of dishes are minimalist: "Tomatoes" and "Halibut." This is odd, because nothing else about Marlow and Sons is straightforward. For starters, there is no one named Marlow. The owner is Andrew Tarlow, who also owns Diner (around the corner). "Escarole" is actually a Caesar-style salad with escarole, breadcrumbs and grated parmesan, which is a good idea—raw escarole needs something biting to tame the bitter taste and thickness of the leaves—but in practice leaves one wishing for crunchy romaine. "Tomatoes" is a large plate of thinly sliced green, red and yellow heirloom tomatoes with basil and shaved Piave, a milder, smoother version of parmesan. The plate is beautiful and bountiful. Other dishes are still more involved, like the exquisitely pan-seared "Halibut," a dish like a Bouillabaisse: the fish fumé perfectly developed in a deeply buttery broth with fresh fava beans and bread for dipping. The crostini changes with the seasons; on this night, it was a smear of ricotta cheese and juicy roasted squash and zucchini, and it was neither over- nor underwhelming—just whelming. The "Brick Chicken," par-cooked under a brick to flatten a breast and thigh then finished in a saucepan, is a fun gimmick that results in a perfectly-done chicken. Most of the food is good, some of it is great and none of it is forgettable.

Many of the wines at Marlow and Sons are organic, biodynamic and unfiltered, yielding a wayward list of old world wines that pair uncannily well with the (somewhat haphazard) but always flavorful food. The service at Marlow is fantastic— efficient, educated, friendly and passionate—so don't hesitate to ask for elaboration of the succinct menu.   TALIA BERMAN

So much of Masten Lake feels unexpected, from the graphic plate presentations to the unusual ingredient combinations. Yet these disparate parts come together to create a distinctive, composed restaurant, thanks to chef Angelo Romano, who, prior to opening his own place, worked at Mario Batali's

MASTEN LAKE
New American
285 Bedford Ave. (Grand & S. 1st St.)
Ⓛ Ⓙ Ⓜ Ⓩ
718 599-5565
No Website
Mon–Fri: 11am–4pm, 5pm–12am
Sat–Sun: 10am–4pm, 6pm–12am

Lupa and Roberta's in Bushwick. At Masten Lake, Romano focuses on seasonal ingredients and bold flavor combinations, all paired with biodynamic wines.

The Catskills-inspired restaurant is airy-yet-cozy with exposed brick walls, a lengthy bar and a small open kitchen. Generous hunks of Italian bread finished with sea salt and olive oil arrived first. While tearing off bites, we considered Masten Lake's concise menu, divided into cheese, cold, hot, pasta and protein. We started with Summer Snow, a mellow sheep's milk cheese from Woodcock Farm, VT, reminiscent of brie. Our cold dish arrived as long slices of firm, vibrant green cucumber tousled with slightly salty leaves of purslane, creamy straciatella cheese and pieces of smoked trout. Our hot selection, prawns, quickly followed; sizable and toothsome, they had a hint of char that married well with a smear of salty squid ink and sweet roasted green figs. Next came house-made cappellacci, stuffed pasta shaped like the Pope's hat. In this case, the al dente cappellacci were filled with a light and fluffy mix of monkfish, zucchini and mascarpone—we loved the texture but wished for a bit more filling. Before long, another substantial dish was set before us: pink slices of duck with chanterelle mushrooms and spicy farro topped with a creamy, soft-cooked duck egg. We weren't wowed by the duck itself but loved the dish as a whole, particularly when the tasty farro combined with a bite of egg and duck—another nod to the chef's keen sense of composition.

SARAH AMANDOLARE

THE MEATBALL SHOP
Italian
170 Bedford Ave.
(N. 7th & N. 8th St.) Ⓛ
718 551-0520
themeatballshop.com
Sun–Wed: 12pm–2am
Thu–Sat: 12pm–4am

Naming a restaurant after a single item can be a tricky endeavor—yet the Meatball Shop confirms there is an exception to every rule. This no-fuss restaurant from co-owners Daniel Holzman and Michael Chernow elevates meatballs with ingredients like fennel seeds, prosciutto and ricotta.

Sitting down at a sturdy, wooden table I couldn't ignore giddy expressions of fellow diners experimenting with playful flavor combinations. Jars of markers and laminated menus set a whimsical tone as I colored between the lines, pairing a classic beef herb-packed meatball with a chili-laced tomato sauce and a hearty veggie ball of green lentils with a thick mushroom gravy. Right as the volume of choices seemed overwhelming, our cheery server broke down the dishes, defining the quirky (and sometimes suggestive) names.

First up: naked balls. This is a meatball classicist's dream—nuances of heat and herb shine through in four unadorned meatballs. I was transported back to my grandmother's Italian kitchen with the 'smash' sandwich—two meatballs smashed inside toasted brioche. A word of caution: order this when eating with the kind of company that won't mind sauce dribbling down your chin. Butter lettuce, sweet-roasted parsnips, chickpeas and you guessed it—meatballs—combine to form the vibrant 'everything but the kitchen sink salad'. We raved about flawless sliders including chicken and pesto. Side dishes were a bright counterpoint to hearty meat dishes, such as a lightly-dressed arugula and sliced apple salad or crisp steamed broccoli.

I would have preferred a two-top instead of squeezing into the center of a communal table—but one bonus was feasting our eyes on neighbor's selections. Ingredient-conscious customers can happily devour beef from Creekstone Farm and Heritage pork. The Meatball Shop's delicious food and whimsical atmosphere reminded me that sometimes, it's perfectly delightful to play with my food.   JESSICA COLLEY

After a successful two year stint as chef de cuisine at Manhattan's Mercadito Cantina, Ivan Garcia headed across the river to open up his first restaurant—Mesa Coyoacan in Williamsburg. Named for the area of Mexico City where he grew up, this authentic Mexican cocina honors the region's culinary classics with time-honored recipes handed down by Garcia's grandmother.

MESA COYOACAN
Mexican
372 Graham Ave.
(Skillman Ave. & Conselyea St.) Ⓛ Ⓖ
718 782-8171
mesacoyoacan.com
Mon–Wed: 5pm–12am
Thu–Fri: 5pm–1am
Sat: 12pm–1am
Sun: 12pm–12am

The restaurant's industrial-looking Graham Avenue facade disguises a warm inviting interior that features dim filament light fixtures, a seating medley of cozy booths, high-tops and communal tables, and pop music bouncing off the walls. On the night of our visit, patrons packed into the bustling bar area to sip fresh fruit sangria and margaritas made with house-infused tequilas.

With a focus on organic ingredients and quality proteins, the menu offers excellent Mexican fare and street-food staples. There are plenty of healthier choices, including my ceviche of tender octopus, grilled corn, avocado, pico de gallo and orange slices in a spicy jalapeño citrus infusion, and tiny handmade tortillas (three tacos to an order) topped with spit-grilled chunks of marinated grass-fed beef, chopped onions and cilantro. The roasted organic chicken arrived smothered in a flavorful pipian (traditional Mexican verde sauce) of pumpkin seeds, tomatillo, chiles and zucchini. However, the chiles en nogada entrée—a roasted poblano pepper stuffed with shredded Berkshire pork, pears, apples, peaches and almonds, covered with luscious walnut sauce—was the dinner's clear high point. The balance of sweet, savory, creamy and nutty was absolutely exquisite.

By delivering high-caliber ethnic eats in a swanky space, Mesa Coyoacan has quickly become a neighborhood hotspot. So grab a date or a group of friends and settle in for some delicious comida that does granny proud. MEGAN MURPHY

MIRANDA
Latin American, Italian
80 Berry St. (@ N. 9th St.)
718 387-0711
mirandarestaurant.com
Mon–Thu: 5:30pm–10:30pm
(Closed Tue)
Fri: 5:30pm–11pm
Sat: 12pm–3pm, 5:30pm–11pm
Sun: 12pm–3pm, 5:30pm–10pm

Mustard walls, exposed brick alcoves, paper cutout banners, straw-seated chairs and tin lanterns—Miranda speaks Latin American romance with an extra accent: Italian. Mauricio Miranda and Sasha Rodriguez built Miranda from a lifetime of Latin cuisine and extensive experience in Italian kitchens.

They translate foreign flavors through local products, sourcing most ingredients from New York's Rondout Valley and farmers markets. The result is an eclectic menu, amenable to all types of eaters. Facilitated by a rich vegetable broth, they're happy to make once-meaty dishes vegetarian upon special request.

The food's Italatino identity doesn't slap you in the face. It eased us in, first with a salad of market greens, spiced beets, ricotta salata and marinated mushrooms, which found sweet acidity in light sherry vinaigrette. Ceviche is a mainstay at Miranda, adapted to what's in season and at market. Our visit saw wild fluke marinated with melon; the outcome was refreshing, though too-small cuts made it difficult to appreciate the seafood's flavor.

Well-diversified, handmade pastas are available as appetizers or entrées. The "ñoqui verano," potato-carrot dumplings with summer vegetables and cotija cheese, sounded more exciting than they tasted. I've met good small gnocchi and great soft gnocchi before, but these were too much of both.

Pan-seared Long Island duck breast got the Miranda treatment, surrounded by creamy polenta, Tuscan kale and chile de arbol sauce. The combination's soft quirk peaked my palate's interest, though each element alone—from the chile to the duck itself—was rather mild. A plate of grilled branzino with organic quinoa, roasted red peppers, gaeta olives and capers owed its distinction to the puzzling, earthy warmth of achiote (annatto seed) oil.

Brooklyn's the kind of place where locavores and foodies with wanderlust can find equal solace. Together, they'll find satisfaction at Miranda. JACLYN EINIS

Korean for "gathering," Moim serves the kind of food you'll want to linger over with friends. Geometric lounge stools, sleek wooden banquettes and slate brick walls dotted with dark wooden sushi platters speak modern zen. The serenity extends to Moim's elegant back patio, where straight lines and natural elements personify the chef/owner Saeri Yoo Park's contemporary take on Korean tradition.

MOIM
Modern Korean
206 Garfield Pl. (7th & 8th Ave.)
② ③ ④ Ⓑ Ⓠ
718 499-8092
moimrestaurant.com
Tue–Thu, Sun: 5:30pm–10pm
Fri–Sat: 5:30pm–10:30pm

Park brings her Korean upbringing and New York City training to the kitchen for impressive results. She utilizes local and sustainable ingredients in light interpretations of the dishes she grew up on. Our well-meaning but not-so-well-versed waiter couldn't tell us much about any of this, but his smiles kept us in good spirits.

Four skinny summer rolls united julienned carrots and zucchini within the snappy crunch of a delicate radish wrapping. Our next foursome was the vegetable dumplings. Earthy shiitake and enoki mushrooms, mild kimchi and vegetable protein burst at the seams of an almost translucent, sumptuously gummy dough.

We moved from umami to sweetness with the Dak Gui, a Korean-spiced organic half chicken. Served with a molasses-tinged sauce, fingerling potatoes, carrot and Korean jujube (a chestnut-like fruit also known as the Chinese date), the chicken was roasted to fried-like crispness. An updated take on the classic bi bim bop, our Ya-Cha Dol Sot Bi Bim Bob mixed seasonal market vegetables, mushrooms and organic tofu on a chili-spiced bed of multigrain sticky rice. Intentionally al dente azuki beans mixed well with the toothsome rice, which featured a perfect soccarat (the delightful crust imperative to perfect paella).

Park's food is affordable and accessible, but she isn't looking to drive the K-Town throngs with grill-it-yourself and all-you-can-eat gimmicks; it's refined touches on Korean classics that has in-the-know Brooklynites gathering at Moim.   JACLYN EINIS

135

MOMO SUSHI SHACK

Japanese
43 Bogart St.
(Grattan & Moore St.)
718 418-6666
momosushishack.com
Sun–Thu: 12pm–3:30pm,
6pm–10:30pm
Fri–Sat: 12pm–3:30pm, 6pm–12am
(Cash Only)

Not to be mistaken for a member of the David Chang family, this Momo's nearest kin is Williamsburg's Bozu. Discreetly housed in a former garage, the sleek, dimmed space's small size and long communal tables will have you rubbing elbows with Bushwick's artfully inked arms.

Our first pick from Momo's roster of vegetarian eats was the tofu salad: extraordinarily silky pressed tofu, avocado, local heirloom tomatoes and watercress were artfully plated and drizzled with basil-infused soy sauce. Dishes arrived as they were ready, and our Wagyu burger came next. The seared beef improved with each bite from the crumbly periphery to a tartare-like center. Spinach and shimeji mushrooms soaked up the beef's broth; while wasabi mashed potatoes arrived in a bowl all their own, they sadly lacked a real wasabi kick. That kick appeared in meal's surprise starlet, the Pork Betty doused soft, thinly sliced Heritage Foods pork in a delectable sauce of sake, soy, wasabi cream and cilantro.

Twelve fish-on-rice "bombs"—think nigiri but rounder—united for the Party Bomb (I would have liked a brown rice option). Tuna bombs topped with spicy mayo and wasabi cream packed the greatest punch. The only organic fish was a bland Scottish salmon, which shone brighter as a uni-topped starter than in the Pink Bomb. We circled back to veggies with the tasty Katide Doko Roll, an umami bomb of crimini, shitake and avocado. A mediocre mix of chopped vegetables, cilantro and spicy tofu mousse, the Rami Roll tasted more succotash than sushi.

I enjoyed mixing the three types of soy: classic, slightly spicy and green with wasabi (tamari is available as a gluten-free alternative). A fun twist on the classic ginger palate cleanser, Momo's is yuzu-pickled red cabbage.

Momo is ideal for family style dining, but this hidden spot is no secret; large groups should be prepared for a (worthwhile) wait. JACLYN EINIS

Natural Village Café, a mostly organic and completely kosher restaurant, has an airy space with a slight cafeteria feel, featuring a number of white tables and wooden chairs, walls of manufactured stone tiles, a dessert counter and bright lighting. Artificial green plants sit on every table and a large painting of what looks like Jerusalem hangs front and center.

NATURAL VILLAGE CAFÉ
American, Mediterranean
2 Ave. I (@ Dahill Rd.) Ⓕ
347 417-6424
naturalvillagecafe.com
Mon–Thu: 9am–8pm
Sun: 10am–9pm

The café serves vegetarian-and vegan-friendly food alongside a few fish entrées. The menu spans salad options to appetizers, sandwiches to paninis and spelt pizzas to vegetarian pastas—and more.

According to the menu, The Mediterranean Plate should include falafel balls, eggplant, hummus, tahini and Israeli salad. Ours arrived without the eggplant and tahini (the restaurant ran out), but it was still delicious; the small falafel balls were lightly seasoned and far from greasy, and the hummus was fresh with a refreshing tang. The Grilled Halumi Salad with romaine, grilled halumi, tomatoes, cucumbers and red onions and mushrooms sautéed in a "state-of-the-art" teriyaki sauce was pleasantly interesting; though an unusual pairing, the sautéed veggies worked well with their fresh counterparts.

The Village Pizza is topped with mushrooms, onions and two types of mozzarella on a thin spelt crust sprinkled with sesame seeds. The veggie toppings were nestled under the melted cheese, and the spelt flour crust left nothing to be desired.

Our favorable eats took a hit, however, when the wild salmon with lemon and garlic arrived. Overdone and extremely lemony, the flavors were too pungent and somewhat stale. Happily, the accompanying sides of grilled vegetables and baked sweet potato redeemed the dish; they were the ultimate meal favorite. The sweet potato was expertly prepared, and it perfectly complemented the thinly sliced, seasoned and olive oil-coated grilled vegetables.

While Natural Village's cafeteria ambiance is not quite traditional, you'll be glad they've put their innovative twists on classic fare that leave you feeling healthy yet satisfied.   AMY SUNG

NILE VALLEY ECO-JUICE AND SALAD BAR

Fast Food
138 Willoughby St.
(Flatbush Ave Ext. & Albee Sq.)
Ⓑ Ⓓ Ⓝ Ⓠ Ⓡ ② ③ Ⓐ Ⓒ Ⓖ
No Phone
No Website
Daily: 10am–8pm

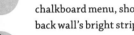

Located in Downtown Brooklyn's Dekalb Market, Nile Valley Eco-Juice and Salad Bar, like all other food stands and storefronts here, is housed in an old shipping container. Unappealing? It's actually the complete opposite. Colorful shipping containers and a laid-back yet creative vibe with food—and shopping to match—set the tone for Nile Valley, a 100 percent vegan eatery serving juices, smoothies, Jamaican patties, salads, wraps, burgers and raw food made with local and organic produce.

As we examined the menu taped to the window (there's also a chalkboard menu, showcasing specials and other options), we noticed the back wall's bright striped pattern of red, green and yellow. Even-livelier fabrics featuring eclectic patterns were being sported at Nile Valley, and combined with the DJ playing music and the covered outdoor picnic seating, the energy was contagious.

We ordered the delicious and carefully constructed walnut "tuna" wrap. First, a leaf of lettuce is laid on the wrap, then the finely chopped walnut salad is scooped into its cradle—genius to prevent a soggy wrap. Also filled with shredded carrots, tomatoes, red cabbage, cucumbers and some avocado, the substantial wrap satisfied us as much as (if not more than) our fond-but-now-distant memories of real tuna. The increasingly regular special, live raw pizza—a dehydrated nut/seed crust topped with tomato sauce and cashew nut cheese and layered with bell peppers, red onions, sprouts and avocado—is also a must-try.

Simple salads are also offered, such as the Avocado Basil Salad with Annie's Homegrown sesame ginger dressing. Fresh basil arrives from the vegetable garden located on the Willoughby side of the market, which Nile Valley contributes compost to.

Nile Valley had this carnivore thinking, if I could eat this food every day, maybe being a vegan would be easy after all.　　　AMY SUNG

Husband and wife team Paris Smeraldo and Meg Lipke call their restaurant Northeast Kingdom, the very romantic-and-important-sounding name for the northeast corner of the state of Vermont, their home state. Other than their origins, it's not quite clear why Smeraldo and Lipke chose this name for their restaurant on the soon-to-be-gentrified corner of Brooklyn off the Jefferson stop on the L train, but then again, not too much about Northeast Kingdom–the restaurant–is entirely clear.

NORTHEAST KINGDOM
New American
18 Wyckoff Ave. (@ Troutman St.) Ⓛ
718 386-3864
north-eastkingdom.com
Mon–Wed: 6pm–11pm
Thu–Fri: 6pm–11:30pm
Sat: 11am–4pm, 6pm–11:30pm
Sun: 11am–4pm, 6pm–11pm

Upon entering, one may be greeted, one may not. A glass of wine might be generously poured, or it might look skimpy. A carrot salad with farm greens, peanuts and nam prik pla (a classic Thai dressing translated as "chili fish sauce") has delicious vegetables but no perceivable spice, fish sauce, or really anything Thai-inspired. Happily, the food is mostly delicious; potted vegetables, a revolving sample of the season's bounty, featured a simple and satisfying succotash with picalilli on our visit. Fried green tomatoes are quite tasty as well, crusted with cornmeal and served with thick, sweet grain mustard vinaigrette and a pickled egg.

After making selections from the menu, one might discover that there are a couple of chalkboards posted around the restaurant touting nightly menu additions. There you will find their beef burger, veggie burger and possibly a pasta dish. Nothing was particularly memorable about the pasta, but do not miss the spicy cracked black bean burger, served with guacamole, cheese and some kind of tomato-based spicy sauce that complements the burger perfectly. The bun is fantastically doughy with airy holes like a dense focaccia. The fish of the day, priced by the market, is often the most expensive thing on the menu, but if fish is what you want, it is certainly worth it, because someone in that kitchen knows how to cook it.

TALIA BERMAN

O-CREPES
French
147 Front St. (Pearl & Jay St.)
718 715-4460
o-crepes.com
Daily: 8am–7pm

Open since March 2010, O-Crepes is a tiny and easy-to-miss creperie on the now-developed Front Street. The small space features a yoga-studio-esque ambiance with exposed brick, low lighting, trance-y cultural music playing in the background and bamboo mats covering the windows to its neighbor. As a fast and casual creperie, O-Crepes only seats about six between three small tables.

The menu offers sweet and savory crepes as well as a build-your-own crepe option, and unexpectedly, three varieties of Vietnamese sandwiches and one flavor of bubble tea. The produce is organic, chicken is free-range and the ham used in crepes is organic, while the ham in the banh-mi is just antibiotic and hormone-free.

The ham banh-mi was surprisingly delicious with perfectly crusty bread, pickled radish and carrots, cilantro and mayo (with sriracha sauce if you order it spicy). The tofu version was less flavorful; plain silken tofu was a healthy ingredient but made for a soggier sandwich.

On the crepe side, original flour, buckwheat and gluten-free crepes are available. While gluten-free was unavailable when we visited, we sampled both the original and the buckwheat. The Architectural Digest crepe featured free-range chicken, mushrooms, onions and Swiss cheese. Incredibly savory and tasty, this was more than enough to satisfy as an entire meal. The Yoga Sun crepe with mushrooms, tomatoes, spinach and feta was much lighter. We couldn't get enough of the warm, crumbly feta with the healthier tasting buckwheat crepe, even if it was a touch drier than the original. We ended our meal with the Apple Pod, a simultaneously simple and scrumptious sweet crepe with apple slices, crushed walnuts and honey.

While minimal in décor and space, O-Crepes' doesn't miss a beat with its crepes—and banh-mi—which follow suit in pleasing (delicious) simplicity.

AMY SUNG

On a leafy residential corner in Fort Greene, an oasis hums with activity. Groups share pan-Mediterranean tapas and sangria. Romance blooms over oysters at a table for two. Locals dine solo at the bar, book in hand. Slowly turning ceiling fans, dark wood benches with ikat-patterned cushions and potted trees suffuse the room with tranquility.

OLEA
Mediterranean
171 Lafayette Ave.
(Adelphi St. & Clermont Ave.)
Ⓐ Ⓒ Ⓖ ② ③ ④ ⑤ Ⓑ Ⓠ
718 643-7003
oleabrooklyn.com
Sun–Thu: 10am–4pm, 5pm–11pm
Fri–Sat: 10am–4pm, 5pm–12am

That calm vibe comes in handy, because the food is plenty exciting on its own. Whatever else you order, don't skip the fried olives. Meaty, oversized green beauties are breaded and fried, piled atop fiery harissa and cooling tzatziki. This is a snack to inspire cultish devotion. Chilled organic yogurt soup studded with zucchini, plump golden raisins and walnuts, speckled with herbs and sprinkled with brick-red ground sumac, sounds too weird to work—and yet our spoons didn't stop scooping until they scraped the bottom of the bowl. Only the chicken empanadillas fell short; a pair of deceptively lovely crusts enclosed dry, flavorless filling.

At first glance, farro pasta inspired curiosity more than excitement. In a terra cotta dish, ruffled brown noodles tangled with julienned zucchini, thin spears of asparagus and sweet peas, all topped with a dollop of Salvatore ricotta and a handful of garlic chips. It looked… healthy, in an I-should-eat-this way. But the riot of flavors—astringent, mellow, nutty, sharp—and the rumble of textures—velvety, sturdy, crisp, airy—put this firmly in the want-to-eat column. I barely looked up, which was fine with my dining companion, who was so distracted by his organically-raised rib eye, topped with garlicky pimenton butter and a jumble of greaseless shoestring fries (paired with an addictively spicy ketchup), that he didn't even notice.

Go to Olea for a date, a celebration, or a casual dinner. Between the Casablanca atmosphere and the inventive menu, it's an accessible escape.   DEBBIE KOENIG

ORTINE
Italian
622 Washington Ave.
(Pacific & Dean St.)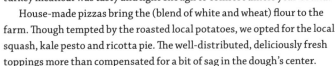
718 622-0026
ortine.com
Mon–Thu: 5pm–10pm
Fri: 5pm–11pm
Sat: 10am–11pm
Sun: 10am–10pm

A burst of charm on a relatively dull stretch of Washington Ave., Ortine is every bit as unexpected as its location. White tin ceilings and oilclothed tables lend a country-homey feel to the small café. Up front, a mini wooden bar features Kombucha, a shortlist of affordable wines (some organic) and rotating local beers curated by co-owner Steve Guidi. The back patio plants diners in the middle of Guidi and wife/co-owner Sarah Peck's kitchen garden.

The couple's homegrown organic cuisine is wholly original; it's what they love without regards to what a menu traditionally looks like. The result? Eclectic, approachable food with an Italo-barnyard slant.

After complimentary spiced popcorn, hearty salads bode well as a light main or shared appetizer. Ortine's nicoise –featuring Acme (Greenpoint's smoked fish mecca) smoked trout, marinated anchovies and wedges of house cured pickles—was a refreshing take on the classic, but the sum of its parts a bit salty. The yellowish pickles seemed omnipresent, appearing in our entrées' side salads as well as an impressive—if slightly over-oiled—salad of golden beets, walnuts and pear.

Entrées warmed the heart without clogging the arteries. A light lasagna paired thinly sliced mushrooms, gooey parmesan and house-made mozzarella cheese. The lovechild of matzo balls and stuffed turkey, our turkey meatloaf was tasty and light enough to comfort diners year-round.

House-made pizzas bring the (blend of white and wheat) flour to the farm. Though tempted by the roasted local potatoes, we opted for the local squash, kale pesto and ricotta pie. The well-distributed, deliciously fresh toppings more than compensated for a bit of sag in the dough's center.

Not sure exactly what you want? Go to Ortine to strike a balanced between quality and value, laid back and attentive service and quirk and simplicity.

JACLYN EINIS

Armed with great taste and a smile, Alex Palumbo brings the food of his native North Italy to North 6th. Edison bulbs and raw brick walls with metallic accents lend a rustic-modern feel to Osteria Il Paiolo, while the open space and attentive-but-not-overbearing service make for a relaxing setting.

OSTERIA IL PAIOLO
Italian
106 N. 6th St.
(Berry St. & Wythe Ave.) Ⓛ Ⓖ
718 218-7080
ilpaiolonyc.com
Mon–Fri: 12pm–4pm, 5pm–12am
Sat: 11am–12am
Sun: 11am–11pm

The menu deserves to be treated the Italian way: an order from each course. As you eat your way through the top of Italy's boot, rest assured that your food was sourced much closer to home, much of it from the Bronx Greenmarket. Our journey began with the insalata di barbabietola. We've all seen beets and goat cheese cohabitate before; what stood out about this salad wasn't flavor but rather freshness.

It's hard to choose just one carb at a restaurant named for the copper pot (il paiolo) used to prepare polenta. Choose from the polenta shortlist or sink your teeth into perfectly al dente pasta. Most pastas are made in house, like the sumptuous chocolate pappardelle with wild boar ragu and vegetables. Savory bites of meat (some a touch dry) complimented the cocoa and Sambuca-infused sauce's subtle sweetness. A simple eggplant and tomato orecchiette would have been overshadowed by the pappardelle's novelty had it not been so tasty.

A simple grass-fed buffalo steak was lean and perfectly seasoned, served alongside an arugula salad with bright lemony dressing. The more dynamic "lamb two ways" paired a tender thyme-crusted rack of lamb with a house-made lamb sausage; studded with parsley and spices, the soft merguez was a scene-stealer. A healthy serving of sautéed broccoli rabe rounded out the dish.

Having spent five years working the front-of-the-house at Da Silvano, Palumbo knows how to treat his regulars. Make sure to introduce yourself when you go—you'll be back.   JACLYN EINIS

PALO SANTO

Latin American
652 Union St. (4th & 5th Ave.) Ⓡ
718 636-6311
palosanto.us
Mon–Fri: 6pm–12:30am
Sat–Sun: 10:30am–3pm, 5pm–10:30pm

Before any of Jacques Gautier's Latin American market cooking hits your lips, simply mouthing words from his menu is delicious: Asopado de Mariscos. Cazuela de Hongos. Palo Santo occupies the ground floor of a brownstone in Park Slope where the menu changes daily. Each piece of recycled paper showcases Chef Gautier's seasonal inspiration. Mellow Caribbean music, exposed brick walls and a garden where fresh herbs grow wildly complete the down-to-earth vibe. Paintings by local artists adorn the walls, offsetting brick with scenes of ocean and sky.

Maybe these paintings inspired my first choice of the evening, a refreshing watermelon salad. Juicy cubes of watermelon were tossed with queso fresco, slivers of red onion and just-picked mint. I couldn't resist pork tacos when I learned every tortilla is made to order. Stuffed with succulent pork, guacamole and crisp sliced radish, these tacos were playfully served on a skewer. Tuna ceviche next captured my attention. Lime, chili paste and cilantro leapt off the plate with each mouthful of tuna. There is something lighthearted about Chef Gautier's cuisine, even regarding presentation. Pan roasted bluefish topped with salsa verde arrived on a bright green stripe of a banana leaf. Sweet plantains were the star of this dish, caramelized on the outside, melting under the slight pressure of a butter knife. The grand finale was grass-fed skirt steak, artfully topped with garlic scapes—some stretching over a foot in length. Despite adornments, it was the marinade, expert sear and medium rare temperature that mesmerized with each bite. Some customers might lament that a favorite dish comes and goes too quickly on the daily-changing menu, while others will return eager to see what the chef has up his sleeve next. It seemed to me that at Palo Santo there are no precise rules or recipes—only passionate cooking from the heart.

JESSICA COLLEY

Fusing Greenmarket produce with upscale Southern cuisine, Peaches redefines casual comfort food in a big way. Not your typical stick-to-your-ribs soul food spot, this approachable Bed-Stuy eatery features a menu of lighter, more refined fare and updated Cajun classics. Take a walk down tree-lined Lewis Avenue, and you'll be charmed by the warm and inviting

PEACHES
Southern
393 Lewis Ave.
(Decatur & MacDonough St.) Ⓐ Ⓒ
718 942-4162
peachesbrooklyn.com
Mon–Thu: 11am–10pm
Fri–Sat: 11am–11pm
Sun: 10am–10pm
(Cash Only)

space filled with art covered bright yellow walls, hanging paper lanterns and pillow-rimmed window bench seats you'll want to cozy up to.

Chef-owners Ben Grossman and Craig Samuel source locally and use organic, antibiotic- and hormone-free proteins whenever possible. Farm fresh salads highlight seasonal produce, like our plate of juicy heirloom tomatoes, grilled peach wedges and subtle farmer's cheese that screamed summer when kissed with sweet balsamic vinaigrette. When a big bowl of fluffy Southern-style grits arrived, I expected more gusto from the blackened catfish fillet on top; happily, the flash-broiled Creekstone Farms rib eye entrée packed a serious flavor punch with just a touch of scallion-lime butter and a stir-fry of chopped zucchini, onions, peppers and tomatoes. Balancing out the many meat and fish dishes were several vegetarian options, including a side of tender sautéed spinach tossed with sliced garlic and an impressive entrée of hearty seared portobellos, creamy goat cheese and grilled onions layered between doughy ciabatta bread—a sandwich sure to please herbivores and carnivores alike.

The staff was friendly and accommodating, yet the pace of service was quite slow on the night of our visit; our server more than made up for it with a sincere apology, charismatic smile and cornbread on the house. But before you settle into serious Southern comfort, hit up an ATM, as this is a cash only establishment. All things considered, our experience at this charming neighborhood café was just peachy. MEGAN MURPHY

PETIT OVEN

French, New American

276 Bay Ridge Ave.
(Ridge Blvd. & 3rd Ave.) Ⓡ
718 833-3443
petit-oven.com
Wed–Thu: 5:30pm–10pm
Fri–Sat: 5:30pm–11pm
Sun: 5pm–9pm

Worthy of a trip to Bay Ridge, the intimate Petit Oven touts a menu equally refined in size and flavor. Seasonal ingredients drive the weekly selection of roughly ten à la carte items and a three-course tasting menu (from which diners may select individual plates).

Inspired by her childhood on a Polish farm, Chef-owner Katarzyna Ploszaj (a.k.a. "Kat") decided to "Grow it. Cook it. Eat it." in New York. We began the latter with the (not so) spicy market greens. Despite the misnomer, the salad was on point, tossed with bit of roasted radish, velvety goat cheese and sweet balsamic. While a fluke ceviche refreshed with subtle sweetness and spice from melon, pineapple and jalapeno, it was the pork that left a lasting impression. A few indulgent bites of the braised belly were just enough; the melt-in-your-mouth meat was perfectly paired with a ginger- and cilantro-spiced bean cassoulet.

Petit Oven's mains speak to every appetite with a daily steak, local chicken, house-made pasta and salmon burger as some of the usual suspects. While a crisp-skinned sole meuniere main was beautifully seasoned and cooked perfectly, its bland side of jasmine rice could have benefited from a stronger hit of its promised saffron. With a generous coating of arugula-basil pesto (the leaves just picked from the chef's garden), the pillowy house-made gnocchi were so divine, it was all we could do not to lick the bowl clean.

Wise diners will coordinate their visit with that of the cloudlike dumplings. Though with a little oven this good, Kat might have you in Bay Ridge on a weekly basis. JACLYN EINIS

For a place that is called Prime Meats, they sure love their vegetables—and so will you. Salad after salad is delicious. Some have spicy radishes, others bitter greens, still more with crunchy seeds, and all are laced with zippy vinaigrettes. The beet salad is particularly fantastic and features

PRIME MEATS
German
465 Court St. (@ Luquer St.) F G
718 254-0327
frankspm.com
Mon–Fri: 10am–Close
Sat: 8am–Close
Sun: 8am–Close

the root two ways: roasted and pickled. The beets are garnished with grapefruit and pine nut brittle—first an acerbic element and then one richly sweet—to counteract the soft flavor of the beets.

Other menu items are equally wonderful. The pickle-brined chicken breast, served with pulled thigh meat and fingerling potatoes, is a neat preparation; the pickle juice brine is salty but not overwhelming. The daily fish is generally prepared with lemon, salt and olive oil—fresh, clean flavors that express "simple" at its best.

Unsurprisingly, the menu is dominated by various incarnations of meat, and they are uniformly generous, delicious and, well, meaty. Each meat smacks of the animal from which it came. Pork chops, thick cut bacon, pork belly—all are decidedly porky. Steak frites, Côte De Boeuf, the burger—these items are unmistakably beefy, rich and minerally, almost as if you can taste the iron content. Slow-braised beef brisket is hearty and heartwarming. Steak tartare is among the neighborhood's best, a coarsely chopped Creekstone sirloin intensely accented by mustard oil, Tabasco, anchovy, capers and shallots. The organic grilled pork chops are enormous, juicy and succulent, served with a piquant pickled pepper jus.

Prime Meats is the carnivorous expression of Frank Castronovo and Frank Falcinelli, owners of Frankies Spuntino in Manhattan, Frankies 457 down the street and Pedlar coffee shops. With each new venture, the Franks are able to enlarge their network of purveyors, most of whom are local, organic and sustainably-minded.   TALIA BERMAN

PURBIRD
American, Fast Food
82 Sixth Ave. (@ St. Marks Ave.)
② ③ ④ ⑤ ⓓ ⓝ ⓡ ⓑ ⓠ

718 857-2473
purbird.com
Tue–Sun: 12pm–10pm

Pete and Christina Lekkas understand that sometimes "less is more." Perched on the corner of Sixth Avenue and St. Marks Place, the couple's Purbird is all about chicken: hormone- and antibiotic-free, Amish farm raised, vegetarian fed, free-range chicken.

Patio stones lead from the wraparound front patio to the small white brick-tiled interior. The space is cozy and clean enough for dining in, though the "fast slow food" lends itself to takeout.

Purbird delivers for free to neighboring Brooklyinites and on its promise of "Brooklyn's best flame-grilled, all natural chicken." Extraordinarily juicy and grill-marked throughout, the restaurant's signature dish is everything you could ask for in a bird. De-boned (aside from one unobtrusive anchor) and brined, it's finished with olive oil, lemon and herbs—a balanced seasoning that enhances the meat's natural flavor. You can add your choice of organic house-made sauce like the quince chutney, zucchini raita or roasted lemon and parsley, though I was satisfied leaving mine undressed. Served with warm pita, the half chicken makes for an ample and affordable dinner for two, though I'd happily order the whole to ensure leftovers. Round out the meal with wholesome sides like the three-cheese whole-wheat mac & cheese or an unfussy vegetable of the day (barely-spiced, grilled zucchini, for instance).

You can get your grill fix sandwiched with the whole-wheat chicken thigh wrap or otherwise sate carnivorous cravings with house-ground chicken burgers and sausages. Several salads, like a chop of lettuce, beet, pepper, feta and chickpea (tossed with a light, if overzealously applied, balsamic) provide sizable vegetarian alternatives (available with a chicken breast or thigh).

Purbird's home has seen a number of restaurants come and go, but as long as the Lekkas keep getting the basics right, they'll be roosting in Park Slope for a long time to come.

JACLYN EINIS

Even with a Prospect Heights address, Rawstar Café will transport you far away from city life. With its friendly, laid-back vibe, this tiny tropical café exudes positive energy and sports bamboo walls, a flurry of eclectic décor and a mishmash of seating—from tables to couches to stools. There's even a small counter tucked under a tiki-like grass roof.

Run by a close-knit Trinidadian family (all practicing vegans themselves) who put "heart and soul" onto each plate, Rawstar features "raw vegan Caribbean food" made from nuts, seeds, vegetables and fruits. Admittedly, not one of my first dining choices—I'm an omnivore and tend to like my food warm—I managed to enter with an open mind (and empty stomach).

First up, a chipotle hand roll of fresh veggies, pecans, plantains and coconut in a thin nori wrapper spiced with a chipotle aioli, was a surprisingly delicious kick off to the meal. My salad of hearty kale leaves coated in creamy nut cheese was another solid starter, but the spinach cheese puffs missed the mark. The pizza deluxe with a crunchy dehydrated nut crust, layer of Sun–dried tomato relish, diced vegetables and sweet pineapple was really tasty, but even more impressive was the somewhat inside-out veggie burger. Two dense, chewy nutmeat patties sandwiched around greens and flavorful macadamia nut sauce proved to be a standout. Don't miss the curry plantains—smooth and sweet with mild yellow curry spice and Caribbean-flair.

During my visit, only half of the menu items were available, since Rawstar is transitioning to a constant rotation of dishes. If you're craving crowd favorites like the burger or lasagna, just call ahead. Don't forget to bring some green; it's cash-only. Pleasantly surprised by my raw Caribbean adventure, I left feeling enlightened, relieved and most importantly, full.   MEGAN MURPHY

RAWSTAR CAFÉ
Caribbean
687 Washington St.
(St. Marks Ave. & Prospect Pl.)
② ③ ④ ⑤ Ⓢ

718 975-0304
rawstarnyc.com
Tue–Sat: 2pm–11pm
Sun: 2pm–10pm
(Cash Only)

ROBERTA'S PIZZA
Italian, New American
261 Moore St.
(White & Bogart St.)
718 417-1118
robertaspizza.com
Daily: 11am–12am

Dining at Roberta's is about more than just eating. In addition to the two dining rooms, there are two bars—one outside, the other in, a greenhouse, a private events space, a radio broadcasting station—Heritage Foods Radio—and a pizza oven. Dining is communal, and the menu is pizza-focused, rounded out by a generous selection of salads, salumeria, pasta and entrées from the kitchen—none of which quite measure up to the standard set by the pizza. Slightly thinner than its competitors', it is crunchy, salty, and airy as only the best crust can be. Roberta's suggests various combinations of toppings, often involving a pork product (prosciutto cotto, speck, pork sausage), sometimes a vegetable (kale, portobellos, brussel sprouts) and always cheese (taleggio, parmigiano, mozzarella). Or create your own pizza from the list of toppings on offer: among them potatoes, capers, jalapeno and artichokes. Whatever you choose, the crust will be the same, and that is where it counts.

Aside from pizza, the best items at Roberta's are the salads. They are fairly modestly portioned but creatively composed with exciting ingredients. Shaved sunchokes with parsley, anchovy and Consider Bardwell rupert—an aged jersey cow's milk cheese that tastes somewhat like gruyere—is nicely balanced and a delicious way to enjoy sunchokes. Kohlrabi with mascarpone, black garlic and blood orange is also remarkable if only for the colors on the plate. From the kitchen, pappardelle with duck and tomato sofrito is intensely flavored but not gamy, and the snapper is fresh and bright with cucumbers, mandarins and castelfranco olives.

Roberta's sources ingredients from nearby farms (some even within the borough), and the menu changes as the seasons do. But be warned before making the trek out to Bushwick: big as it is, it's insanely popular, and you will have to wait.

TALIA BERMAN

Who knew "cheese" could taste so… alive? The folks at Rockin' Raw, that's who (the cheese is dairy free, of course). The lovechild of a New Orleanian and her Peruvian husband, Rockin' Raw is a welcoming ode to Creole, Peruvian and raw cuisine under the peaceful glow of Mardi Gras beads.

Slide through the narrow dining room to enjoy your meal in the back garden (don't worry, it has beads, too). Settling in wrought iron chairs in the shade of fig and apple trees felt more like visiting a friend's summer hideaway than eating out.

The organic, gluten-free menu is chock full of raw twists on cooked classics like lasagna and crab cakes. I appreciated the in-house pickling of the cayenne-dusted "fried" pickles, though they lacked the crunch I'd hoped for. Heartier than they look, Rockin's nachos top dense, flax chips with tomatoes and delicious sunflower and cashew purees. A tasty—if slightly vinegary—salad of kale, dulse and avocado makes for a leafy introduction to a more seed-heavy meal.

The textural mushroom-based burger gave me falafel déjà vu. The spiced-up patty comes with a side of collard greens and funky-enough-to-try onion "rings" whose texture mimics that of fruit leather or beef jerky, depending on your diet. The highly lauded live zucchini pasta came doused in "pesto," a sweat-your-face-off (and I can hold my picante) pepper-based sauce that I found more odd than enticing.

A long list of naturally sweetened desserts merit a visit all their own. If there's only room for one, make it the mini Raweo, the vegan's moist and creamy answer to Hostess. Do yourself a favor and pair it with a scoop of coconut and almond milk-based ice cream, like fragrant lavender vanilla or nutty lucuma.

Whether you've already unplugged your stove or are simply raw-curious, Williamsburg's Mardi garden awaits you.   JACLYN EINIS

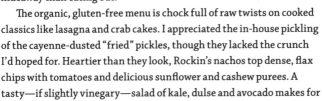

ROCKIN' RAW
Creole, Peruvian
178 N. 8th St.
(Driggs & Bedford Ave.)
718 599-9333
rockinraw.com
Mon–Wed: 4pm–10pm
Thu: 4pm–11pm
Sat: 12pm–12am
Sun: 12pm–11pm

ROEBLING TEA ROOM
New American
143 Roebling St. (@ Metropolitan Ave.)

L G J M Z

718 963-0760
roeblingtearoom.com
Sun–Thu: 10am–4:30pm, 6pm–11pm
Fri–Sat: 10am–4:30pm, 6pm–12am

This seemingly unassuming red brick warehouse produces a surprising array of creative Greenmarket dishes. Once inside, the austere industrial cloak is discarded and reclaimed by flowery wallpaper, ample sunlight and an expansive bar. Most menu items we sampled boasted a delicious balance

of healthful vegetables and their richer, more sinful enhancements. The ravioli was stuffed with crunchy kale and topped with julienned candy striped beets, its high veggie representation accented by poppy seeds and a thin, buttery sauce. Though the same sauce was somehow saltier on the pappardelle entrée, its juicy heirloom tomatoes, softened leeks and tender, fennel-studded chicken meatballs more than managed to come together as a delicious and unique dish. I appreciated the appetizer's generous portion of bok choy, but the leafy stalks tended to dwarf their less corpulent crostini vessels. Together with the preserved lemon and smear of melted butter, the appetizer's construction was more than easy to overlook.

The swordfish torta, a menacing skyscraper of a sandwich, featured a hefty square of grilled swordfish topped with slippery black bean, avocado and chipotle-mayo spreads. Though the black bean and avocado were necessary components — they cooled down the fiery chipotle seasoning — their liberal application slightly overwhelmed the mild fish. Torta quibbles aside, Roebling Tea Room churns out tasty dishes that feature relatively exotic vegetable combinations and robust seasoning.   ALLIX GENESLAW

With crisp white-tiled walls and a marble-topped communal table and bar, Roman's feels more French oyster bar than it does Italian trattoria. But the ever-changing graph paper menu at this little Fort Greene hotspot is all Italian.

ROMAN'S
Italian
243 Dekalb Ave.
(Vanderbilt & Clermont Ave.) Ⓖ Ⓒ
718 622-5300
romansnyc.com
Mon–Thu: 5pm–11pm
Fri: 5pm–12am
Sat: 10am–3:30pm, 5pm–12am
Sun: 10am–3:30pm, 5pm–11pm

Most of that Italian is straightforward and authentic, though some plates are skewed through the lens of the chef's market picks and daily whims (spelt berry soup and veal with sauerkraut, for example). Don't count on returning for your favorite dish (as you might at the owners' skeleton-menued Marlow & Sons and Diner), but bank on discovering a new favorite with each visit. The kitchen puts out only a handful of different dishes each night, and what they do, they do right.

The menu begs to be indulged through (at least) three courses, and we complied. Thick slices of fresh bread offered a stage for our first starter of pole beans and cured swordfish. The wide, gangly beans were the perfect crunch to the salty creaminess of swordfish puree. A fantastic mix of juicy pickled peaches, ricotta and almonds made bitter radicchio sweet as pie.

Though all three pastas (including a vegetarian taglioni spiked with hot peppers and bucatini with anchovies, cabbage and mint) beckoned, we honed in on the classic Roman rigatoncini alla gricia. Pancetta and melted caciocavallo cheese brought a lush smack of salt to the toothsome tubes.

Served with potato puree, a red-wine braised beef shank was moist and tender but not memorable enough to lament its short menu life. The halibut had more finesse, served with squash, saffron and thinly sliced scallops in a soppable scallop both.

With a few white-clothed tables tucked away from crowded communal tables and regulars at the bar, Roman's effortless vibe may deceive you; food this good doesn't come easy.   JACLYN EINIS

ROSE WATER

New American

787 Union St. (@ 6th Ave.)

Ⓓ Ⓝ Ⓡ Ⓑ Ⓠ ② ③ ④

718 783-3800

rosewaterrestaurant.com

Mon–Fri: 5:30pm–Close

Sat–Sun: 10am–3pm, 5:30pm–Close

Clusters of flowers welcome you to Rose Water, a hanging barrier between Union Street and the restaurant's sweet street-side patio. Inside, a petite room plays host to big flavors. Savoy vet John Tucker opened Rose Water in 2000, working with regional family farms long before "locavore" became the RSTLNE of Brooklyn's foodie vernacular.

Rose Water's seasonal menu may be labeled American, but its locally-sourced dishes are flecked with foreign touches. Sautéed to crisp brown perfection, our trenne (penne's cooler, triangular cousin) found ideal mates in sautéed spinach and shimeji mushrooms, whose woodiness complemented the natural sweetness of the accompanying tarragon cream. Ample enough for two, a cucumber gazpacho with bell pepper coulis featured a hit of heat from a drizzle of paprika oil. As refreshing as I found the cucumber-cilantro puree, I felt a tinge of appetizer-envy listening to our neighbors sing the praises of their charred endive and grilled calamari salad.

Using local and sustainable ingredients means adapting with the daily catch. On my visit, wild barramundi stood in for the menu's sea bass. The delightfully bright dish paired the fish with sweet corn succotash, summer squash and Green Goddess sauce (think an über-herbal, minty pesto). I was equally taken by the smoked leg of lamb, whose almost-rare cuts came with tzatziki-esque yogurt sauce and a side of lemony Israeli couscous and broccoli spigarelli.

Rose Water's dependable, fresh fare is well suited for a market menu, which they serve Monday through Thursday. Both the three-course and five-course tastings offer fantastic value and optional wine pairings. With roughly twelve tables, the intimate space fills up a flash; reserve a spot before you go. Your palate–and body–will thank you later.

JACLYN EINIS

Every step nearer confirms your original instinct: you've discovered something special. Tucked in a corner of Boreum Hill's Historic District, plants weave through Rucola's ironworked windows, blanketing an intimate, bustling interior. One of Brooklyn's more

RUCOLA
Italian
190 Dean St. (@ Bond St.) F G A C
718 576-3209
rucolabrooklyn.com
Tue–Fri: 11:30am–4pm, 5:30pm–12am
Sat–Sun: 10am–4pm, 5:30pm–12am

gorgeous takes on rustic farmhouse design, Rucola finds gentle light in milk-bottle-on-wheel chandeliers hanging from weathered wood panels and tea candles set on stacked wooden crates.

No doubt you'll want to take your meal like you're in the restaurant's North Italy muse and linger. Rucola's executing a simple concept well—fresh, local, seasonal Italian. This was clear from our first bite; a salad of the restaurant's namesake bitter green with shaved radish, parmesan featured a light but complex celery seed vinaigrette. Next we traveled south for the caponata, whose eggplant found balance between oil and vinegar, sweet currant, mint and sour piquant capers. It was an enjoyable take on the Sicilian classic but felt sleepy—perhaps a dose of salt by way of nuts would have brought it fully to life.

The strozzapreti, on the other hand, was not for the salt-averse. Brilliant green garlic pesto clung to al dente twists of pasta with Grana Padano and zucchini sealing the dish's success. It was delectable as a split course; all that garlic and salt might have been too overpowering otherwise.

A wonderfully rare Long Island duck came with a perfect garnish of dark cherries, turnips and braised swisSwissrd. The striped bass was pan seared with crispy-flaky-moist precision. Beside it, scallion, pancetta and sweet corn made wild rice taste as exciting as it sounds.

Rucola's support for local agriculture extends beyond the menu. If their farm-fresh Italian isn't enough to keep you coming back on a weekly basis, perhaps This Batch, the flexible CSA they host with partner farms, will do the trick.   JACLYN EINIS

RYE

New American

247 S. 1st St.
(Roebling & Havemeyer St.) Ⓛ Ⓙ Ⓜ Ⓩ
718 218-8047
ryerestaurant.com
Mon–Thu: 6pm–11pm
Fri: 6pm–12am
Sat: 11am–12am
Sun: 11am–11pm

$$$

Though set on South 1st with speakeasy inconspicuousness, Rye was actually designed with pre-Prohibition bars in mind. Dark tin ceilings and mahogany-heavy interior establish a tone of hushed class, equally appealing for a date, a lone drink at the mirror-backed bar or a meeting of the minds along leather banquettes.

Rye's food is as enticing as the space, inviting vegetarians but truly indulging those with a penchant for meat. A delicious endive and pear salad with toasted pecans and cello radish began our meal on a light note, sneaky bits of bacon and blue cheese surreptitiously salting the frisée.

The beet ravioli were an artful stray from the norm. Thinly sliced beets stood in for the usual pasta, cradling spoonfuls of creamy goat cheese and accented by roasted tomatoes, mache, toasted pine nuts and herbal basil oil.

You can't go wrong with a Rye's sandwiches, pleasures made less guilty by way of sustainable meat. Rye's "bacon" sandwich highlights their house-cured and smoked Berkshire pork belly, its charred skin giving way to a center even softer than the focaccia it's served on.

Our roasted duck breast, while flavorful, was a touch chewy. Perfectly seasoned, generous sides of Moroccan couscous, swiss chard and tomato chutney rounded out the dish. The pan roasted skate delivered big flavors along with a delectable crispness and moist interior. Unnecessary olives tainted an otherwise tasty braised artichoke ragout, while simplicity worked for an unadulterated side of (also braised) organic kale.

Seasonal herbs and fresh fruit find their way into several of Rye's old-fashioned cocktails. Paired with comforts old and new, they're just one more reason to start your evening (or weekend morning) like it's 1900.

JACLYN EINIS

Saltie takes a seafaring theme, from the décor—crisp white with nautical blue—to the playful menu names ("The Captain's Daughter"), to the kitchen tucked behind the counter, as small and snug as a ship's galley. With no bathroom and just eight backless stools tucked against two walls, it

SALTIE
New American
378 Metropolitan Ave. (@ Havemeyer St.)
L G J M Z

718 387-4777
saltieny.com
Tue–Sat: 10am–6pm
(Cash Only)

feels more like a dinghy than an ocean liner. But thanks to the owners' inventiveness and respect for ingredients, Saltie is the Queen Mary of sandwich shops.

That respect begins with the bread, which is baked in-house. But Saltie doesn't stop there. Many of the vegetables are grown on one owner's farm upstate. All are organic, as are most of the proteins.

Six of the seven mostly vegetarian sandwiches are served on chewy, salt-flecked, perfectly oily focaccia. The seventh, a vaguely Indian, vaguely Middle Eastern assemblage called the Clean Plate, is built atop spongy, sweet naan. It's served open-faced, layered with chunky, citrusy hummus, bulgur, julienned fresh and pickled vegetables and herbs, drizzled with a dilly yogurt sauce. It's a big stinkin' mess—one that will have you diving for every fallen scrap. More mayhem arrives in the Scuttlebutt, a Greek salad sandwich by way of Barcelona: hard-boiled eggs, feta, olives, capers, pickled vegetables, herbs, greens, tomato, all stuffed inside a plank of focaccia generously smeared with pimenton aioli. Eating it requires all hands on deck, and it borders on too salty, but the swirl of flavors is mesmerizing.

Less successful is the Spanish Armada, a thick slice of potato-and-egg tortilla, which is lovely on its own, but sinks under too much of that smoky aioli. For an eggy sandwich stick with the Ship's Biscuit, nothing more than loosely-scrambled eggs piled atop pillows of salty, creamy ricotta. Rich and simple—like Saltie—it'll satisfy even the most ravenous deckhand. **DEBBIE KOENIG**

SALUD
Latin American
1308 Avenue H
(Argyle & Rugby Rd.) Ⓠ
347 295-1191
saludnyc.com
Mon–Fri: 8am–8pm
Sat: 10am–7pm

The location—on a sleepy Midwood block shared with a martial arts center and a dry cleaner—doesn't promise much. But inside Salud's light-filled, spacious storefront lies a gold mine of inventive, healthy eats. Should Michele Obama retire to open a café in Guadalajara, it'll probably look something like this: vibrant takes on Mexican and American standards featuring organic ingredients, produce by the bushel and a smattering of meat.

Given the owners' Mexican heritage, you might expect that dishes from south of the border would be the star here. Our forks did duel over the authentic-tasting vegan tamale, olive oil-enriched masa dough studded with soft, mildly-spiced vegetables. Cozy and comforting, it feels much less virtuous than it is.

But there are standouts from the north, too; we devoured the house-made veggie burger. With seasoning that hints at falafel, it combines texturized vegetable protein with beets, kale, parsley and more in a patty so tender it nearly falls apart. Even the most basic offerings receive a fresh spin—the peanut butter sandwich beautifully balances a smear of house-ground, barely salty nuts with bananas, thin slices of tart green apple and from-scratch jam (on the day we visited, a delicate, rind-studded orange marmalade) between slices of sturdy multigrain bread.

Juices and smoothies make up half of Salud's menu, and each one we tried was bright, refreshing and filling. Two stood out; a whole organic lemon, pith, seeds and all, gets blended with brown sugar and a splash of water to create a thick, mouth-puckering shake—lemonade, reborn. The Lucha Libre smoothie whirs Mexican chocolate, bananas, peanut butter and rice milk into dessert in a glass.

Given its humdrum surroundings, chances are slim you'll stumble upon Salud. But for vegetarians and vegans especially, it's worth a trip.

DEBBIE KOENIG

Step inside funky-rustic Saraghina, and you'll want to stay a while. The rambling rooms' décor is mismatched but not twee, the garden is downright charming, the staff is welcoming, and the menu— 8 wood-fired, Neapolitan-style pizzas, a green salad and cheese and salumi platters plus an extensive list of Italianesque specials, all made from local or organic ingredients— offers something for everyone.

SARAGHINA
Italian
435 Halsey St. (@ Lewis Ave.) Ⓐ Ⓒ
718 574-0010
saraghinabrooklyn.com
Mon–Fri: 10am–5pm, 6pm–11pm
Sat–Sun: 12pm–4pm, 6pm–11pm
(Cash Only)

Surprisingly, since pizza makes up the heart of the menu, our biggest disappointments came in pie form. The crust, while nicely chewy, needed salt desperately. I struggled to finish a single slice of my Ortolana, San Marzano tomatoes blanketed with mushy, underseasoned eggplant and zucchini and gobs of bland, fresh mozzarella. More enticing was the Capocollo, a tomato-and-mozz pie topped with basil leaves and thinly sliced coppa, spicy cured pork neck from an upstate purveyor. Thanks to that wood-burning oven, the ham's edges crisped up nicely while the centers offered a salty, pleasantly meaty punch.

The ever-changing specials list is a treasure trove—especially the grilled items. Several dishes, including a tender, smoky-charred grilled octopus salad and an unexpectedly excellent burger, are frequently available. Others change with the season. A fabulous grilled apple salad featured wedges of soft, sweet fruit around a brightly bitter snarl of frisée and watercress, scattered with crunchy pine nuts and topped with a tangy dab of goat cheese. Perfectly simple grilled striped bass was paired with asparagus and roasted fennel so melty and mellow, I could've eaten an entire plate of it alone. The juicy pork chop, also grilled, was another example of perfect simplicity, served alongside nothing but lemony bitter greens.

Saraghina proves a basic tenet of Italian cooking: for a memorable meal, use fine ingredients and do very little to alter them.

DEBBIE KOENIG

SAUL
New American
140 Smith St.
(Bergen & Dean St.) **F G**
718 935-9844
saulrestaurant.com
Sun–Thu: 5:30pm–10pm
Fri–Sat: 5:30pm–11pm

$$$

A neutral environment lets SAUL diners focus on what's important: excellent food. With six consecutive years of Michelin stars under his belt, chef Saul Bolton has been at the forefront of Boerum Hill's dining scene since 1999.

Charming photographs of farmers markets adorning SAUL'S menu foreshadow the freshness to come. Don't try to plan your meal online, as selections change with the season. Bolton uses artisanal, organic ingredients to create new American cuisine inflected with Spanish and French flavors.

A primer for our dinner, a double shot of carrot ginger soup tasted as pretty as it looked. Dressed in apple vinegar, heirloom red and golden beets were delicious alongside slightly bitter greens, crisp slices of fennel and apple and toasted hazelnuts. The cool pea soup was as vibrantly colored and luxuriously smooth as our amuse-bouche, owing much to the coconut milk in its base. This green summer treat as delightful as a banana split, with a pimento-infused oil the cherry on top.

At SAUL'S each turn, subtle flavor innovations keep the palate on its toes while allowing the dish's key components to shine. Three large scallops sat buttery soft and perfectly browned on a white bean puree. Chorizo added salt to the sweetness of the caramelized scallops and their accompanying raisin-pine nut mix on kale. Our squab (a young pigeon, one East Coast ingredient I was relieved to learn was not über-local) was pan roasted to a thorough pink. Its silky texture and mild but distinctive flavor were well matched by a grainy green farro, earthy brussels sprouts and cauliflower and baby potatoes in an addictive curried sunchoke puree.

Like Bolton's food, the service is impressive but unpretentious. I can't wait to see what next season's flavors bring to SAUL. JACLYN EINIS

South Brooklyn goes south of the Mason-Dixon line at this sleek Smith Street spot. Inspired by his Arkansas past and the greenmarket of his Carroll Gardens present, chef/owner Robert Newton cultivates refined, contemporary comfort throughout Seersucker. Large windows and a wall of jarred preserves bookend the light space,

SEERSUCKER
Southern
329 Smith St.
(President & Carroll St.) (F) (G)
718-422-0444
seersuckerbrooklyn.com
Tue–Fri: 6pm–10:30pm
Sat: 11am–3pm, 6pm–10:30pm
Sun: 11am–3pm

a white paneled bench running along the whitewashed brick walls. Southern flavors infuse every bite on the menu, though never with a heavy hand.

While many flock to Seersucker for fried green tomatoes and fried chicken, the menu's full of less-guilty pleasures. Our knowledgeable waitress indulged us with the stories behind the sustainably sourced meats. Juicy peaches and pickled cherries sweetened a tasty plate of shaved Edwards and Sons country ham, and our next starter was a celebration of the tomato: huge, ripe slices of jersey tomatoes topped with a softly-curded black pepper ricotta, green tomato relish and a few precious bites of yellow husk tomatoes.

The green onion spaetzle was a fluffy, charming novelty but lacked the savory complexity to truly awaken the taste buds. The trout was more addictive, made crisp by its potato crust and paired with perfectly contrasting North Carolina peanuts, zucchini and sweet and sour tomato. Our sizeable pork chop arrived on a pool of hominy puree with a side of sautéed kale. The slight sweetness of the meat's brown sugar and bourbon brine let its natural flavors shine through. On one hand, I was pleasantly surprised by the refined lightness that pervaded each dish; on the other, the seasonings were so light they failed to leave me craving more.

That said, I'll be back. With an inspired concept and staff, Seersucker sets themselves apart from the other guys on the block. Has Newton made the South taste local, or the local taste southern? However you spin it, it's impressive.

JACLYN EINIS

SIGGY'S GOOD FOOD
New American
76 Henry St. (Pineapple & Orange St.)
Ⓐ Ⓒ ② ③ Ⓝ Ⓡ

718 237-3199
siggysgoodfood.com
Mon–Fri: 11am–10pm
Sat–Sun: 10am–10pm

Siggy's Good Food says it loud and proud with a trademarked slogan: "Organic—Back to Better!" The walls are painted the deep golden yellow of a just-laid organic egg yolk, and their fruits, vegetables, meat and dairy are 100% organic. Quirky menu proclamations (like "Aliens eat free", illustrated with the familiar green face) made me expect the hippy-dippy vibe of old-school health food shops, but the bustling café is utterly contemporary: top-notch, seasonal ingredients in inventive combinations albeit with occasional misfires.

Take the Grilled Baby Artichokes, for example, sliced down the middle and cooked face-down until the tender, interior leaves ruffle up, so crisp they shatter rewardingly between your teeth. The stems are left long, slender and firm, tempting me to pick one up like a wonderfully grassy, vegetal popsicle. Quinoa Spinach Cakes are a beautiful pair of compellingly crusty green disks slathered with bright red salsa, but after the first bite an abundance of cumin overwhelms the dish.

The salmon burger—prepared without fillers, of course!—is spectacular. The patty bursts with flavor from herbs, onions and pops of briny capers, with none of the overwhelming fishiness that elsewhere leads me to regret my order. Creamy avocado slices and a light smear of vegan mayo provide cool contrast to the hot burger and its warm brioche bun. Only one dish truly disappointed: The Eggplant Veggie & Tofu Lasagna's noodle-free premise sounded appealing, but the monolithic, mono-textured slab of mushy eggplant slices, vegan cheese and tomato sauce tasted like that old-school health food with a capital "bleh." More than half remained untouched when we set down our forks.

But one major let-down wasn't enough to overcome the sheer pleasure that comes from dining at Siggy's. It's a happy place, filled with people enjoying their food—and the fact that it's all good for you is a delicious bonus.

DEBBIE KOENIG

In most cases it isn't a good sign to leave a restaurant with a strong taste still on your lips, but the opposite is true of Simple Café in Williamsburg. Stepping out of the sunny corner café, I could still taste smoky eggplant from house-made babaganoush on my tongue. My visit convinced me that this casual café is a spot where I could happily be a regular. A varied menu full of guilt-free, healthy, flavorful options along with the spacious tables and outdoor seating all combine for a welcoming, fuss-free atmosphere.

SIMPLE CAFÉ
New American
346 Bedford Ave. (@ S. 3rd St)
Ⓛ Ⓙ Ⓜ Ⓩ

718 218-7067
simplecafenyc.com
Tue–Wed: 10am–8pm
Thu–Fri: 10am–11pm
Sat–Sun: 10am–8pm

We started our lunch journey to Algeria—homeland of the chef—with a quinoa salad, topped with strips of eggplant and mixed with fresh cilantro, tomatoes and shallots. Next came the addictive babaganoush, smoky bite after delectable smoky bite, scooped up with warm Algerian-style bread. Sandwiches were served on the same house-made bread, crisp on the outside with a delightfully chewy interior. Chicken breast, more smoky eggplant, thick slices of ripe avocado and cilantro were piled on split bread for the hearty Marcy sandwich, served with a lightly dressed salad. Anyone tired of bland sandwich combinations will revel in every bite of the spicy lamb sausage sandwich, complete with peppers, red onion and the zing of harissa sauce. As another imaginative touch, antique jars served as glasses for washing down the spice.

This affordable café strikes a chord with simple flavors done well and items so craving-worthy you will be drawn to return. In the case of Simple Café (and in my opinion): that fragrant, handmade Algerian bread and smoky eggplant.   JESSICA COLLEY

SMOOCH CAFÉ

American

264 Carlton Ave. (@ Dekalb Ave.)

718 624-4075
smoochorganic.com
Daily: 8am–9pm

It's amazing what you can do with good, organic ingredients and a quartet of panini presses and hotplates. Just ask the guys behind the counter at Smooch, a Fort Greene coffeehouse/rec room where laptops abound and the vibe is so low-key there's no sign out front. From this kitchenless space they turn out a dozen breakfast-all-day dishes plus a handful of lunchier sandwiches and salads.

That laid-back attitude comes in handy, since just making sense of the menu—with cheeky, incongruous item names like "The Most Sultry Sandwich in Brooklyn or My Names [sic] Not Hugh Phaqah" (a tofu Panini) and "Sexy Venezuelan Toast" (supposedly accompanied by the thong of a former Miss World)—takes a while. But once the über-fresh, mostly excellent food arrives you won't care what your dish is called.

Smooch has a knack for flavor combinations. The Birdy Yum Yum, for example, is a turkey panini made unique—and memorable—with a smear of sweet-tart tomato and plum chutney, tender spinach leaves and mellow, melty provolone. A salad called The Voluptuous Vixen actually lived up to the moniker: thick, juicy, ruby-red slices of beefsteak tomato and creamy avocado encircled lime-dressed salad greens, all topped with a mound of lush, piquant hummus. A sprinkling of cracked black pepper and gomasio (Japanese sesame salt) added an alluring crunch—the only thing missing, oddly, was bread for scooping hummus.

Audacious names failed Smooch only once: The Exceptional Omelet was anything but. Beaten eggs enclosed a slab of cream cheese and raw sliced tomatoes rendered watery by the heat, while too-thick jalapeno rounds scorched our tongues, obliterating all other flavors.

Just as smooch is an amusing term for an intimate, sexy act, Smooch is an intimate, sexy place with a lighthearted demeanor, perfect for whiling away an afternoon.   DEBBIE KOENIG

There is a lot to live up to in a restaurant called Soigne, (pronounced swan-yey) a French word meaning polished, elegant and sophisticated. This New American restaurant in Park Slope personifies the spirit of this word with extraordinary attention to detail. Everything is designed for the guest's comfort and pleasure,

SOIGNE
New American

486 6th Ave. (@ 12th St.)

718 369-4814
No Website
Wed–Thu: 5pm–10pm
Fri–Sat: 5pm–11pm
Sun: 11am–3pm, 4pm–9pm

from the plush chairs to flickering tea-lights on wood tabletops to artistic arrangements on the plate.

The market-driven menu is composed to deliver outstanding tastes of the season. During our visit, that was a roasted peach salad, a study in contrasting textures with micro arugula, crunchy almonds and just a touch of creamy Great Hill blue cheese. The "bites" section of the menu offers small plates designed to share, including rock shrimp rolls: three split top house-made rolls filled with shrimp, herb remoulade and the crunch of shaved cornichons. Some entrées are also generous enough to share, including the Jurgielewicz Farm duck breast, pan roasted and paired with goat cheese-infused polenta (adorably served its own Le Creuset baking dish) along with honey-roasted figs and a drizzle of port wine glaze. Although this dish is served over spinach, it is a little light on veggies, so go ahead and order a side of roasted carrots for a splash of extra color. Lighter market-inspired entrées include an expertly seared Long Island striped bass, served over English pea puree and fragrant roasted carrots. A handful of crispy Yukon gold gnocchi add more substance.

Soigne should also mean thoughtful—if the atmosphere, flavors and plating all had one thing in common beyond sophistication—they were all thoughtfully imagined and executed. So much so, despite the delicious food, I was inspired to slow down and really admire the polished work before digging in.

JESSICA COLLEY

STONE PARK CAFÉ
New American
324 5th Ave. (@ 3rd St.) Ⓡ Ⓕ
718 369-0082
stoneparkcafe.com
Tue–Thu: 11:30am–2:30pm,
5:30pm–10pm
Fri: 11:30am–2:30pm, 5:30pm–11pm
Sat: 10am–3:30pm, 5:30pm–11pm
Sun: 10am–3:30pm, 5:30pm–10pm

It is hard not be immediately attracted to Stone Park Café in Park Slope with its exposed brick walls and corner across-from-a-park location. An outdoor patio calls for balmy summer nights while the relaxed interior with flickering candles is well suited for a long winter evening. Add to that the fact that Stone Park Café masters the concept of being able to adapt to your mood. Feeling like bold flavors? Pair a small plate of grilled octopus with chorizo, fingerling potatoes and preserved lemon with a main dish of a center cut pork chop with smoked cranberry beans, spaghetti squash and braised mustard seed.

On the night of my visit, a mood struck for something fresh and comforting. I started with the shredded chard salad, enlivened with parmigiano reggiano, lemon and extra virgin olive oil—a delightful little starter. I couldn't resist the short rib slider, a perfect single serving of creamed spinach, smoky short rib and quail egg sitting atop a house-made potato roll. Next came the Giannone farms chicken, moist and tender, served over fresh, house-made tagliatelle with woodsy seasonal mushrooms and bright spinach—nourishment and comfort all in one bowl. The meaty texture of Lake Erie-caught Walleye pike was a lovely counterpoint to Mediterranean flavors of the chickpea puree, black olives and pine nuts.

Stone Park Café nails the 'perfect corner café' market with a relaxed and helpful staff, interesting art (an ink print of striped bass was so fascinating I was compelled to ask about its background) and a spectrum of dishes from adventurous to classic. The dessert menu might lack naturally-sweetened options, but entrée portions are ample. With the first smoky bite of short rib, I knew Stone Park Café was much more than just a pretty face.

JESSICA COLLEY

A stone's throw beneath Lafayette Avenue, a 40-foot cherry wood bar begs Fort Greeners to sit down, relax and have a glass (or better yet, a flight) of wine. Settle into Stonehome Wine Bar's unpretentious lounge-like dining room or make your way to the romantic garden out back.

STONEHOME WINE BAR & RESTAURANT
New American
87 Lafayette Ave. (@ S. Portland Ave.)
Ⓖ Ⓒ ② ③ ④ ⑤ Ⓝ Ⓡ Ⓠ
718 624-9443
stonehomewinebar.com
Daily: 5pm–12am

A wine bar with more to pair than charcuterie and cheese (though they have excellent selections of both), Stonehome boasts a menu eclectic enough to match its extensive wine list (unfortunately, no wines were biodynamic or organic when we visited). Starters range from light—a simple green salad with extra virgin olive oil—to the intense (think curry-rubbed slow roasted pork spare ribs with kohlrabi-carrot slaw and honey-mint glaze). We opted somewhere in the middle, digging into a versatile rose and jersey tomato "Greek" salad. The combination of olives, cucumber, dill and crumbly goat milk feta was delicious but would have benefited from more substantial chunks of tomato or a bed of greens to decrease the saltiness.

Diners fare better with the house-made ricotta ravioli served with hon shimeji mushrooms, sweet corn and parmesan in just-sweet-enough sage brown butter sauce. Sweet corn also came into play as a puree with the spice-rubbed Berkshire pork tenderloin. Served with sautéed green beans, bits of peach and a peach-bourbon jus, the tender pork brought a little smoke, a little more sweetness and a lot of comfort to the table. A salsa verde of capers, cilantro and red pepper topped a likewise generous portion of wild striped bass. Accompanied by a light salad of fennel with dill, the fish was refreshing, if a bit wanting in moisture and intrigue.

Whatever you're in need of—be it light and crisp, rich and complex—Stonehome has a seasonal cure. The trick is deciding which comes first: the wine or the food.

JACLYN EINIS

SUN IN BLOOM

American

460 Bergen St.
(5th & Flatbush Ave.)

② ③ ④ ⑤ Ⓓ Ⓝ Ⓡ Ⓑ Ⓠ

718 622-4303
suninbloom.com
Mon–Fri: 9am–7:30pm (Closed Tue)
Sat–Sun: 10am–5pm

Light pervades Sun In Bloom, from its soothing setting to its invigorating cuisine. A white-walled oasis just a few stroller-dodges from Park Slope's 5th Avenue, the aptly named café is great for healthy take-out and even better for relaxed dining out.

Shelves offer a welcome alternative to smartphone companionship with books on holistic living. SIB'S food is likewise holistic: 100% organic, gluten-free, vegan, Kosher and either raw or raw optional.

Liquid remedies run the gamut from pressed Norwalk juices to nut mylks and smoothies. Vinegar adds a touch of tart to the Acai Crunch Smoothie, a delicious puree of soy mylk, berries, banana and live granola. A not-so-sweet Sweet Lady Green is a vitamin boost of kale, collards, romaine, cucumber, celery and parsley.

A lighter shade of green, the cool purifying Raw Alkalizing Soup joins cucumber, avocado, parsley, romaine, garlic, lemon, salt, olive oil and kangen (alkalizing) water. Jalapeño heats up another cool soup of carrot, lime and ginger.

The Bella Devine salad sprinkled kale flakes and rye-bread-evoking caraway seeds over fresh kale (perfectly "massaged" in live sesame ginger dressing), sunflower sprouts, not-too-sour Sauerkraut, dulse and "sultry smooth" avocado. Though divine, Bella won't sate the ravenous; make her heartier by adding a sprouted Ezekiel wheat wrap ($1). A tangy lemon vinaigrette made my Rockin' Veggie (live hummus, marinated bell peppers, cucumbers and cabbage) sing. The refreshing crunch of the collard green wrap (you can also choose wheat) and small side of romaine infused the dish with a welcome crispness.

Naturally sweetened treats ended the meal on a high note. Get your agave fix with the likes of a scrumptious leMon–blueberry cupcake or a rich chocolate-espresso torte with a strip of mint and crispy cookie sandwich.

SIB says they make their food "in a conscious kitchen with love." I certainly felt the love.

JACLYN EINIS

There are some restaurants that evoke jealousy from the moment you walk in—a jealousy that this restaurant isn't closer to home. Superfine is the type of place where you would gladly become a regular, one that lures you inside with discerning music choices, exposed-brick walls and room between

SUPERFINE
Mediterranean
126 Front St. (Adams & Jay St.) Ⓕ
718 243-9005
No Website
Tue–Fri: 11:30am–3pm, 6pm–11pm
Sat: 12pm–3:30pm, 6pm–11pm
Sun: 11am–3pm, 6pm–10pm

tables. The menu changes slightly each day, reflecting availability of the freshest ingredients. Some might find the menu presented on a hand-written whiteboard charming, while hungry diners might find waiting for an available board frustrating. This frustration is sure to subside when your dishes arrive straight from the chef from the open kitchen.

My meal began with the house salad of crunchy greens, lightly dressed and sized to share. Buttermilk meatballs offered depths of flavor with ingredients like leeks, tomato and gorgonzola. Complete with garlic toast, this dish has all the appeal of a childhood favorite reinvented, yet fell short with a lack of seasoning. The grilled pizza was packed with flavor from meaty crimini mushrooms, tomato and mozzarella with a lovely char from the grill that conjured memories of summer. This DUMBO restaurant specializes in a super-fine upgrade on the classics, like a juicy pork chop with garlic-mashed potatoes (for soaking up gravy on the plate) alongside grilled zucchini. Grilled mahi mahi was served with Yukon gold potatoes so crisp on the outside and melty on the inside, they could have been roasting all day. The dish was kept light with an accompanying bok choy, fennel and green bean salad.

Plates offer simple and clean flavors that could have been prepared in a friend's kitchen (albeit one with serious cooking skills)—they have that kind of unfussy soul. When the craving strikes for meat, potatoes and vegetables, you will find each well executed at Superfine. It's almost like Mom used to make—if Mom used organic poultry, pork and grass-fed beef.

JESSICA COLLEY

SWEETWATER

American
105 N. 6th St.
(Berry St. & Wythe Ave.)
718 963-0608
sweetwaterny.com
Mon–Thu: 12pm–12am
Fri: 12pm–1am
Sat: 11am–1am
Sun: 11am–12am

At first glance, everything about Sweetwater suggests it serves only old fashioned confections -- the gold lettering over the windows, pressed tin ceilings, fleur de lis wall pattern and mosaic tiled floors are examples of such nostalgic flair. Based on the decor, the "sweet" in its name could easily refer to egg creams, malteds and rootbeer floats that were popular in days of yore. When the food is served, however, it is clear that the restaurant's vocabulary is hardly limited to one dessert-related adjective. "Creamy" can be used to describe the poppy seed dressing that blanketed a beet salad. The sweet, purple discs were accented by tangy boucheron cheese and crisp hazelnuts. An arugula salad also contained cheese, but in fried form. Grapefruit, cranberries and the light vinaigrette gave this salad its summery feel, which was certainly appreciated in the height of an oppressive heatwave.

"Juicy", "tender", "homey" and "delicious" seemed to be the evening's buzz words for the protein dishes. The burger, perhaps the menu's best kept secret, was one of the best I've tasted so far in New York. The English muffin proved a competent vehicle for the impossibly juicy meat, which was topped with sweet caramelized onions and cheddar cheese. Both the hanger steak and pork tenderloin arrived steeping in their own robust jus. With its supple mashed potatoes, the fork-tender pork brought to mind a comforting, one pot meal. Kale, which retained its bite, and lightly battered onion rings, airy and addictive, accompanied the medium rare steak. The delicious dishes we sampled more than modified my initial thoughts. Sweetwater is not a gimmicky, one-trick pony but rather a versatile restaurant that serves memorable and well-executed meals. ALLIX GENESLAW

Dimly lit and reminiscent of a romantic cellar in an old Spanish ship, Tabaré sits alone on a quiet block in Williamsburg. Vintage bottles line rustic shelves placed high up on the walls of this Uruguayan restaurant, and the walls, made of various sizes of wooden planks jutting out in varied increments, create the illusion of an ark of sorts. The mood feels subdued yet lively in the seductively cozy space which also features a backyard.

TABARÉ
Uruguayan
221 S. 1st St.
(Driggs Ave. & Roebling St.)
Ⓛ Ⓙ Ⓜ Ⓩ

347 335-0187
tabarenyc.com
Mon–Thu: 5pm–11pm
Fri: 5pm–12am
Sat: 12pm–12am
Sun: 12pm–11pm
(Cash Only)

We started with a range of appetizers, including a roasted beet salad with toasted pistachios, ricotta salata and mint—one the night's favorites. We expected a tossed salad, but were presented with a round plate displaying a single layer of sliced beets, each topped with the ricotta, pistachios and one mint leaf—a caprese-style presentation that was nothing short of delicious.

Of the cheese and spanish tuna empanadas, I favored the tuna, which was moist with a filling of perfect consistency and flavorful black olives that weren't overpowering. The gruyere and fontina empanada included caramelized onions, which made it sweet, savory and cheesy all at the same time; be warned, it was decadent with a lot of cheese.

With pasta being a Uruguayan staple, we had to try the handmade ravioli of the day; fingerling potatoes and fresh mozzarella in a butter sauce. Despite the fact that the dish sounds rather heavy, this was a welcome addition to dinner as a lighter entrée to share. Following the beet salad's lead, five raviolis were splayed on the plate, each with its own piece of shaved parmesan.

Other options like the octopus casserole and grass-fed churrasco were extremely tasty and succulent but fairly oily. Still, Tabaré stays true to Uruguayan home cooking in combining simple ingredients with a Uruguayan flare to create flavorful dishes.   AMY SUNG

THIRSTBARÀVIN

French, New American
629 Classon Ave.
(Atlantic Ave. & Pacific St.) Ⓒ Ⓢ
718 857-9227
thirstbar.blogspot.com
Tue–Thu: 6pm–11pm
Fri–Sat: 6pm–12am

In every way, Thirstbaràvin is a function and a product of its community. This wine bar on the northeastern tip of Prospect Heights came about as a communal effort; a customer at Thirst Merchants, Thirstbaràvin's sister retail wine store, offered the building for rent to owners Emilia Valencia and her husband Michael Yarmack. Their olive oil, a deliciously nutty and earthy first press from southern France, is made by another customer. And yet another patron recommended consulting Brooklyn chef Ginevra Iverson (from Prune in NYC and Eloise in the Bay Area) to develop the menu that changes daily based on market offerings. Valencia and Yarmack's total commitment to Baràvin is rooted in their philosophy: supporting sustainably produced food and wine with minimal intervention both in cultivation and delivery.

The food is simple and slightly French: light sautés, warm bean salad, chilled market vegetable soup. The burrata with ratatouille is a sensational idea both for the balance of texture and the concept; acidic ratatouille complements creamy burrata, and the dish is almost excellent—if the burrata was colder, the vegetables not slightly overcooked and a tad fewer onions, it would be perfect. The warm lentils tossed in the aforementioned olive oil with lemon, lardons and a hard-boiled egg is tasty enough if a little boring, but one cannot overemphasize an appreciation for al dente beans. The surprising stunner of the menu might be the roast beef, served cold with creamed escarole, a marriage that ends well in the mouth, especially when you make your own "involtinis," wrapping the chilly sliced beef around steaming bitter and cheesy greens.

The priority at Thirstbaràvin is clearly wine, and the list features gem after gem of organic, biodynamic, unfiltered, terroir-driven old world wines. But Valencia and Yarmack are committed to excellence, so look for improvements all around.   TALIA BERMAN

The food at Thistle Hill is at once bar food, upscale market-to-table cuisine, and vegan-friendly coffeehouse fare, which makes for a lively—if a little unfocused—dining experience.

THISTLE HILL TAVERN

Gastropub, New American
441 Seventh Ave. (@ 15th St.)
347 599-1262
thistlehillbrooklyn.com
Mon–Fri: 12pm–4pm, 5pm–11pm
Sat–Sun: 11am–4pm, 5pm–11pm

Crispy eggplant with heirloom tomatoes is a hearty plate, softened by French feta, which is creamy, light and far less briny than Greek feta. The vegan chopped salad is filling as well, with seasonal vegetables held together by a very wet dill-dijon vinaigrette, making more of a slaw than a salad—in a good way. The grilled market beans are deliciously charred but served with perhaps slightly too much lemon aioli. Zucchini fritters are little round puffs from the garden with thick crusts and airy insides. The house-made pickles are good enough, impressively crunchy and full of flavor.

The grass-fed strip steak is the priciest item on the menu at Thistle Hill, and it is also the most delicious. Modestly sized and simply grilled, the beef is flavorful and toothsome (like the best beef is). It is served with a ragout of seasonal vegetables that acts as a welcome burst of winter, spring, summer, or fall. As vegan burgers go, theirs is quite delicious, tasting of white beans and white button mushrooms on a soft potato roll, but beware of adding cheese—it overwhelms the delicate bean flavor. The grilled rainbow trout is also lovely, served with a tangy salsa verde to which the crispy trout stands up nicely.

Thistle Hill Tavern occupies a fairly quiet corner on 7th Avenue in Park Slope. Take your time enjoying the food and gaze out the large windows over the avenue. The restaurant is a little further down from the bustle by 9th Street, but with South Slope fast becoming a dining and outing destination, you never know what you might see.

TALIA BERMAN

TRAIF
Southern, New American
229 S. 4th St.
(Havemeyer & Roebling St.) Ⓛ Ⓙ Ⓜ Ⓩ
347 844-9578
traifny.com
Tue–Fri: 6pm–2am
Sat–Sun: 11:30am–3:30pm, 6pm–2am

According to Wikipedia, "traif" is "any food that is not in accordance with Jewish law." More commonly, "traif" is "anything considered vile and non-kosher in the Jewish faith." To chef-owner Jeremy Marcus, Traif is everything he was unable to eat as a kid and, perhaps not surprisingly, everything he wants to eat now. It is also the name of his restaurant.

Pork and shellfish are the basic categories of "traif" food, and Chef Marcus pays homage to both in an exciting menu that changes with the seasons but holds onto a growing roster of plates that are quickly becoming neighborhood favorites. Among these are the ambrosial strawberry-cinnamon glazed baby back (pork) ribs, rich and sweet in the best way possible. The pulled pork BBQ sliders are simple and delicious, served with a modest handful of crunchy sweet potato fries. The salmon and scallop entrées are excellent in a simple seared preparation, served with a seasonal vegetable accompaniment. Have the roasted carrots, which are sweet and al dente and marry well with sunflower seeds, feta, spinach, oranges and grapes. Also try the tuna tartare, which are actually little scoops of tartare atop fried disks of eggplant and flavored with kecap manis, an Indonesian soy sauce, thick and sweet with deep yeasty flavor.

Dine at the bar counter if there is room, where you can watch Chef Marcus churn out hundreds of tiny plates at an alarmingly calm, speedy and efficient pace. Dishes are mostly affordably priced, so it is easy to try many items without emptying your wallet. Portion sizes are similarly on the small side—which is a good thing, because the chef is not afraid to intensify his food with all manner of truffle, egg and porcine supplements. Dine at Traif, and you will be thrilled that Chef Marcus is breaking tradition.   TALIA BERMAN

Urban Rustic is a great idea. It is a deli, it is a grocery store. It is a juice bar. It is a place to study. It is a place to socialize. In the order line, chattering heads tip upwards to navigate the enormous menu scrawled across the walls above the open kitchen and cashier station.

URBAN RUSTIC
American
236 N. 12th St.
(Driggs & Union Ave.) Ⓛ Ⓖ
718 388-9444
urbanrusticnyc.com
Daily: 9am–8:30pm

With an order of eggs, a sandwich or salad, a smoothie or perhaps a burrito, you get a named photograph of either an employee or a famous person to perch at your table so your server knows where to bring your food.

The food is good. The "Cascade" sandwich, grilled chicken with mozzarella, roasted peppers and lettuce, is impressively served on house-made bread, but the chicken is pre-cooked, lending a slight "deli window" flavor to the sandwich. The "Power Wrap," with egg whites, spinach, roasted pepper and your choice of turkey or veggie sausage in a spinach wrap is a sizeable portion with turkey sausage that actually tastes like turkey, which is nice. The burritos are perfect and standard: enormous, hot, spicy and filled with countless choices including steamed and shredded chicken breast and guacamole. The juice bar has a wide selection of the usual suspects with a bent toward vegetables, including ginger, parsley and kale. Smoothies are more indulgent, with options that include soy milk, almonds and vanilla ice cream (gasp!).

Prices at Urban Rustic are...rustic. Virtually everything is under $10, and many breakfast options are under $5. Dishes come garnished with a small and lovely green salad dressed in a tart balsamic vinaigrette—a perfect accompaniment to the universally large portions at Urban Rustic.

TALIA BERMAN

THE V-SPOT

Latin American

156 5th Ave. (Douglass & Degrew St.)

Ⓓ Ⓝ Ⓡ Ⓑ Ⓠ ② ③ ④

spreadvegan.com

Tue–Fri: 12pm–10pm
Sat: 11am–10pm
Sun: 11am–9pm

Over lunch, tables around me mused at the name: The V-SPOT. While some theories bordered on the suggestive, other diners were insistent that it simply means the spot for vegans. This Park Slope restaurant on a busy block of 5th Ave is strictly vegan with influences that reflect the Latin heritage of owner Danny Carabaño.

Inside the sunny front door, exposed brick, cozy booths and no-frills service all set the tone for a casual meal. The V-SPOT might be strictly vegan, but that doesn't mean choices are limited. In fact, the large menu offers an appealing variety that can sometimes be a challenge to narrow down. Stay away from fried options; instead, stick to fresh flavors like those found in the raw nori rolls. The dish features tasty ginger-almond pate along with spinach, carrots and cucumber. Served with chopsticks and slivers of pickled ginger, it is a fresh and flavorful spin on sushi. We were also intrigued by the kale tostadas. Two toasted corn tortillas are topped with raw kale, black beans, avocado and a dash of hot sauce for zing; make sure your water glasses are topped up for this spicy and hearty dish.

Entrée options are equally flavor-packed, especially the 'classic bacon cheeseburger'. The V-SPOT's version includes a veggie patty of lentils and black beans topped with organic tempeh bacon, daiya cheese, crisp lettuce, tomato and red onion on a toasted whole-wheat bun. Served with a side salad, the alternative to a classic burger was filling and tasty. I was equally impressed with the curried kale and quinoa; the spice of a generous portion of ginger-flavored organic quinoa was cooled by sweet sautéed coconut-curried kale and chickpeas. At the V-SPOT, expect creative veggie-centric dishes to take off in surprising and delicious directions.   JESSICA COLLEY

The Vanderbilt is one of Brooklyn's intentionally-designed "late-night" restaurants. The music is loud, the seating is mostly barstool (except in the back where tables can accommodate larger parties), and the kitchen is open to display Vanderbilt's cooks in all their tattooed glory. The menu is geared toward after hours dining, with an emphasis on small plates and an in-house charcuterie program. Midnight snackers rejoice; the food is invariably excellent.

THE VANDERBILT
Gastropub
570 Vanderbilt Ave. (@ Bergen St.)
Ⓑ Ⓠ Ⓐ Ⓒ ② ③

718 623-0570
thevanderbiltnyc.com
Mon: 6pm–11pm
Tue–Fri: 6pm–12am
Sat: 11am–3pm, 6pm–12am
Sun: 11am–3pm, 6pm–11pm

Chef-partner Ben Daitz, who has worked with owner Saul Bolton (owner of Michelin-starred SAUL Restaurant in Carroll Gardens) and most recently Num Pang Sandwich Shop, is responsible for the uniformly well-seasoned, interestingly-combined and almost always delicious creations on offer at the Vanderbilt. The ubiquitous shishito peppers (little green peppers where 1 in 5 is spicy) are just as good here as anywhere, and the smell of them blistering in a wok nearby only adds salivation to the lively atmosphere. The summer bean salad, with slippery wax and green beans, toasted pistachios, yogurt and pickled shallots is addictively good. Also, try the Chatham cod with summer pistou. The pan-seared fish is light, flaky white and generously portioned.

From the charcuterie, the grilled merguez sausage is succulent, gamy and fairly lean, the intense flavor balanced by house-made pita that tastes of the grill and a nicely chilled raita. The snacks are slightly underwhelming: the cauliflower was over-cooked and over-seasoned, and the house pickles are a little boring—but the (impressively, house-made) jerky is delicious. Many late-night diners want French fries and chicken wings, and the Vanderbilt has both—cottage fries and Togarashi-spiced fried wings—but for those of us who crave vegetables, lean protein and balanced flavors in the wee hours, the Vanderbilt is a perfect home away from home.

TALIA BERMAN

VINEGAR HILL HOUSE
New American
72 Hudson Ave. (Water & Front St.)
718 522-1018
vinegarhillhouse.com
Mon–Thu: 6pm–11pm
Fri: 6pm–11:30pm
Sat: 11am–3:30pm, 6pm–11:30pm
Sun: 11am–3:30pm, 5:30pm–11pm

Replete with mismatched vintage flatware, weathered wood floors, chipped stucco walls and a tangle of tumbleweed-cum-chandelier, Vinegar Hill House is archetypically haute-barnyard. Such country chic charm makes for an ideal neighborhood hangout. Yet the crowd—filling the tightly-packed, salvaged wood tables and sweet back garden, sitting at the wooden bar overlooking the deconstructed organ made whiskey shelves and spilling onto the sidewalk out front—clearly hails from beyond Vinegar Hill's three-block radius.

The food, much of it prepared in the restaurant's cramped but open kitchen's wood-burning stove, is deserving of both hype and wait. Cantaloupe, peaches and tomatoes toasted their ripeness with coriander vinaigrette. Watermelon soup was less a soup and more a work of art; a shallow puddle of refreshing juice found depth in a layer of superb crab salad on a watermelon round. The warm garganelli was a delight; its earthy, thinly sliced chanterelles were the perfect fold for sunny sweet corn.

Vinegar Hill House's signature dish may be the cast iron chicken, but the pork is its masterpiece. A cut above all other hogs, the Red Wattle pork epitomized so many of the meat's most desirable characteristics; its charred skin gave way to a pink center that was tender and lean yet juicy and almost beef-like. Eight generous slices sat beside a mound of cheddar grits, which we would have gladly sacrificed for some green.

Cooked pan-in-stove, a delicious swordfish found more balance in a side of sautéed peppers and eggplant. Bits of walnuts and a cooling yogurt sauce brought the Mediterranean to the Block Island fish.

If you haven't yet found your way to Vinegar Hill, superb seasonal food in one of the quaintest spots (and on one of the quaintest blocks) in Brooklyn should put it on your map.

JACLYN EINIS

A modern day trattoria, Verde on Smith sets the scene with dark wood, crisp white and brick walls and a decidedly un-Italian alt-rock soundtrack. High chairs allow comfortable barside dining while a retractable glass wall makes for optimal people watching. Further back, a polished back garden provides an escape from the bustle of Cobble Hill's restaurant row.

VERDE ON SMITH
Italian
216 Smith St. (Baltic & Butler St.)
Ⓕ Ⓖ Ⓐ Ⓒ

718 222-1525
verdeonsmith.com
Mon–Thu: 5pm–11pm
Fri–Sat: 11am–12am
Sun: 11am–10pm

Verde's menu (apparently as new to our waitress as it was to us) is indeed green; it features Italian fare made with from organic produce, fish and meats. An enjoyable baby spinach salad sweetened middle aged (read: smelly but not stinky) gorgonzola with raisins, nuts—most were candied, though not overly-doused in sugar—and a fig vinaigrette. Smoked buffalo mozzarella tied together the lasagnetta's mortadella and eggplant, though I'd have enjoyed the latter more had it been free from a light but unnecessary breading. The drizzle of sweet balsamic over a plate of fresh beets, grilled leeks and velvety robiolina is the stuff (my) dreams are made of.

Simplicity scores once more with the spaghetti puttanesca, sautéed with a light white wine sauce alongside tomatoes, olives and capers. Sushi grade tuna steak, grilled on the outside and rare within, gets a flavor boost from a cream of balsamic sauce. A yummy side of cannellini beans and a sweetish garlicky escarole was big in taste and size. An easy pick for those craving red meat, what the grilled filet mignon lacked in excitement, it carried in quality and weight. Forgettable mushrooms and a more impressive side of rosemary potatoes balanced out the dish.

Verde's Italian fare, though fresh, may not keep you up at night plotting your return—though I have found myself counting creamy cubes of heavenly robiolina to fall asleep.   JACLYN EINIS

INDEX

GLOSSARY

Berkshire Pork: Berkshire refers to a specific breed of pig that is known for its flavor and texture. It may or may not be raised in a sustainable fashion.

Biodynamic: Most often seen in reference to wine, it is essentially a holistic method of agriculture based on the philosophy that all aspects of the farm should be treated as an interrelated whole, never using synthetic chemicals and relying on ecologically sound farming practices often more stringent than organic requirements.

Factory Farming (AKA Feedlot or Conventional): The process of raising farm animals in confinement at high stocking density, where a farm operates as a factory, a practice typical of corporate industrial farming. The goal is to produce the highest output at the lowest cost and antibiotics must be used to mitigate the spread of disease. Many other risks and moral issues exist as well.

Flexitarian: refers to an individual who is conscious of the type and quality of food they consume but is open to consuming all types of foods from vegetarian to meats as long as the quality is high.

Free-range/free-roaming: refers to animals that have access to the outdoors and are not confined to cages.

Genetic Engineering: process of transferring specific traits, or genes, from one organism to a different plant or animal.

Gluten: The mixture of proteins found in wheat grains that are not soluble in water and which give wheat dough its elastic texture. Gluten is also present in rye, barley, spelt and oat grains and is believed to contribute to digestive disorders such as IBS and Celiac disease.

GMO (Genetically Modified): refers to an organism whose genetic material has been altered using genetic engineering.

Grass-Fed: Grass-Fed Meat refers to meat from animals that have been raised on foraged food such as grasses as opposed to being fed a diet of grain-based food.

Grass-Fed/Grain-Finished: refers to meat from animals that have been raised on grass but given a diet of grain near the end of their life in order to fatten them up for market.

Grass-Fed/Grain-Supplemented: refers to meat from animals that have been raised on grass but fed grain throughout their life in a controlled amount.

Greenmarket: the Greenmarket program runs over 50 farmers' markets throughout New York City with over 230 participating local farms. Many Clean Plates featured restaurants are supplied by local Greenmarkets.

Heritage Foods: Heritage Foods are derived from rare and endangered breeds of livestock. Animals tend to be purebred species near extinction and the method of production used saves the breeds and preserves genetic diversity. The organization Heritage Foods USA exists to accomplish this goal by selling foods from small farms to consumers and wholesale accounts building demand for these animals.

Macrobiotic: refers to a holistic philosophy of living that originated in Japan and focuses on balance. The diet associated with the lifestyle is a strict whole foods pesco-vegetarian (includes fish but no meat or poultry or dairy) approach with an emphasis on grains and Japanese foods.

Niman Ranch: a ranch and network of over 600 independent farmers and ranchers all committed to raising their animals sustainably and free of hormones and antibiotics with 100% vegetarian feeds.

Organic: When referring to produce organic means the crop has been grown, packaged and shipped without the use of synthetic pesticides or fertilizers and are non-GMO (non-genetically modified). When referring to animals it means the animal was raised without the use of hormones or added antibiotics and fed only organic vegetarian feed (no animal by-products).

Pasture Raised: Pasture Raised refers to livestock that is predominantly raised on natural foraged food, such as grasses, as opposed to being fed a diet of grain-based food.

Pat LaFrieda: Pat LaFrieda is a New York City distributor of hormone/antibiotic-free, all natural and 100% traceable meat from various farms in New York State. They also source black angus from Creekstone Farms in Kansas, as well as Amish chicken, veal, and lamb from Pennsyvania.

Pescatarian: refers to an individual who consumes primarily a vegetarian diet with the addition of fish.

Raw Foodist: refers to an individual who consumes a diet of only raw foods (foods not heated above 118 degrees farenheit).

Rooftop Farming: Rooftop farms are dedicated to transforming thousands of New York City's unused rooftops into farms to feed local communities and supply local restaurants.

Satur Farms: A local, long island based family owned farm that specializes in growing vegetables and culinary ingredients. Although not certified organic they are committed to organic standards.

Sea to Table: Fish distributor which connects small, sustainable, local fishermen with chefs by shipping fresh seafood directly from fisheries to restaurants.

Seasonal: refers to the practice of eating or serving foods that are grown during that particular season.

Seitan: often used by vegetarians as a meat substitute for its similar texture and high protein content, it is actually the gluten from wheat boiled in a ginger soy sauce.

Sustainably Raised: Refers to a food (animal or produce) that has been created in a way that has minimal negative impact on the environment.

Tempeh: A food derived from fermenting soybeans and pressing them into cakes.

Tofu: A food made from soybeans, water and a coagulant or curdling agent.

Vegan: Refers to an individual who will not consume any foods derived from an animal.

Vegetarian: refers to an individual who will not eat any foods derived from an animal except for dairy and eggs since it was not necessary to kill the animal to obtain the food.

Vegetarian Feed: Refers to the diet fed to an animal. It means the animal has not been fed any animal by-products and is usually fed a diet of corn or other grains, but not grass.

NOTES